laugh and learn

**95 ways to use humor for more
effective teaching and training**

laugh and learn

95 ways to use humor for more effective teaching and training

DONI TAMBLYN

AMACOM AMERICAN MANAGEMENT ASSOCIATION
New York • Atlanta • Brussels • Buenos Aires • Chicago
London • Mexico City • San Francisco • Shanghai • Tokyo
Toronto • Washington, D.C.

Special discounts on bulk quantities of AMACOM books are available to corporations, professional associations, and other organizations. For details, contact Special Sales Department, AMACOM, a division of American Management Association, 1601 Broadway, New York, NY 10019.
Tel.: 212-903-8316. Fax: 212-903-8083.
Web site: *www.amacombooks.org*

This publication is designed to provide accurate and authoritative information in regard to the subject matter covered. It is sold with the understanding that the publisher is not engaged in rendering legal, accounting, or other professional service. If legal advice or other expert assistance is required, the services of a competent professional person should be sought.

Library of Congress Cataloging-in-Publication Data

Tamblyn, Doni.
    Laugh and learn : 95 ways to use humor for more effective teaching and training / Doni
    Tamblyn.
        p. cm.
    Includes bibliographical references and index.
    ISBN 0-8144-0745-5
        1. Employees—Training of. 2. Humor in business. I. Title
HF5549.5.T7 T256 2002
658.3'124—dc21

                                                                        2002011301

Printing number
10 9 8 7 6 5 4 3 2 1

This book is dedicated with gratitude to every gifted teacher I have been lucky enough to have. It is also dedicated to Doug Ryan, who gave me a chance to grow from a comedian to a teacher. Finally, it is dedicated to Edward De Bono, who inspired me by saying, "Humor is by far the most significant behavior of the human brain."

contents

PART I THE WHAT AND WHY

acknowledgments

First and foremost, thanks to Eric Jensen for talking me into writing this book way back in 1997, and for his continued assistance as it was being written.

Thanks also to Malcolm Kushner, whose many insights and rigorous research on humor in business have long acted as a catalyst to my thinking. And thanks for all your personal help and encouragement, Malcolm. My first book might not have gotten written if not for you.

Thanks to Pat Wolfe of Mind Matters, Inc., who took time from her enormously full schedule to talk with me about the brain.

The team at AMACOM has been wonderful to work with. First, my warmest thanks to Jacquie Flynn for giving so generously of both her time and her superb ideas for improvement; this is a far better book than it would have been without her. Editor Niels Buessem not only polished the book but also "got" it, a fact that must bring moisture to any writer's eyes. Thanks also to Jim Bessent for his patience in the face of deadlines, and to Vera Sarkanj for her work in promoting this book.

And finally, to all those talented comedians at Traffic Safety Taught with Humor, whose creativity and enthusiasm in teaching "violators" will always inspire and amaze me: Thanks for taking the job seriously. It was an honor working with you.

the 95 ways

everybody's

a comic

THE MINUTE people find out you used to be a comedian, they positively burst into life. They move closer; they tell you about their favorite club. They ask, who's your favorite stand-up? Didn't they see you on Comedy Showcase?

And then they always, always do one thing: They tell you a joke. Verily spoke the vaudevillian: "Everybody's a comic."

In 1990, I was instructor coordinator for a San Francisco traffic violator school. Traffic school in California is a sort of penance for speeders and stop sign cruisers—regular folks like you and me. They opt to sit through seven-hour lectures on stopping distances and decapitation, in return for keeping their tickets off the record. It's a little like hell: Lots of people attend, but no one wants to be there. At one point, some of these state-licensed schools started hiring comedians to teach. (Yes, only in California.*)

---

*Although at the time of this writing the idea has also been adopted by Texas and Florida.

In my job I recruited over forty-five professional comedians statewide, and trained them to get their "violators" on their feet teaching each other, using, among other things, original skits, rap songs, and bad celebrity impersonations. At the end of their day in detention, our attendees went away energized, flushed with their own creativity—and sold on driver safety. It was both thrilling and fascinating to see how the simple experience of fun had so completely reversed attitudes. Many learners said things like, "This class should be mandatory," "You are saving lives," and "I'm glad I came." When one person, a lawyer, asked, "Would I have to get another ticket to come back here?" I decided that maybe it was time to take this stuff on the road.

> **"The mediocre teacher tells. The good teacher explains. The superior teacher demonstrates. The great teacher inspires."**
>
> William Arthur Ward, college administrator

Most teachers and trainers believe, either from research or gut instinct, that humor helps people learn better. Relatively few, however, give much time to building this very easy skill.

One reason is that they don't think humor is a "skill" that can be "built." Humor is a gift, they believe; you're either born with it or not. They're almost right. Just a hair off. In actual fact, humor is a gift—and Chapter 4 will prove that you, I, and everyone else, were born with it.

Another reason teachers and trainers resist using humor is that they fear the possible negative repercussions. Maybe they will "bomb." Maybe they will inadvertently make an inappropriate joke. Maybe their topic is too serious for humor. Maybe a humorous, playful audience will be too hard to control. Some of these fears are well-founded. Most, as you will see in reading this book, are not.

Perhaps the most immediate cause for the reluctance to use humor, however, is the simple fact that professional development costs money. When it comes to allocating scarce funds, training managers must think carefully. Sure, speakers' and trainers' evaluation scores may go up when they use humor—but will their listeners actually learn better? Will they make the desired behavior changes? Will they score higher on exams? Will they do better on the job? Is there any proof that humor actually improves retention or retrieval of information? Is humor really an effective teaching tool, or just a feel-good contrivance? Aren't we safer using the budget to build the currently-needed technical skills rather than training trainers to be funny?

This book is written to provide a low-risk, affordable way for teachers, trainers, and speakers to start putting humor to work for them. In the process, however, I freely confess that I hope to lead *all* communicators to an appreciation of how humor can help them convey virtually any topic far more effectively, resulting in substantial long-term benefits for themselves, their listeners, and their organizations. I am confident that readers will be as fascinated as I am by the research that strongly suggests humor fulfills several biological purposes—a major one of which seems to be to make us think and work better. Like every other biological function, humor seems essentially to have been implanted to ensure the continuance of the species.

Okay, after that last sentence you're probably thinking this won't be a funny book to read. Stay with me! Nobody knows better than I how pathetic it would be to write an unfunny book on the subject of humor. Therefore, I herewith offer this personal guarantee: If you don't laugh at least once while reading this book, I will eat a raw Japanese sea urchin. I swear. All you have to do is write.**

And now with that vital issue out of the way, let's get back to the subject at hand.

This book will first clarify what humor is. (Ever notice how much disagreement there is on that point?) Next it will examine why humor should be used in virtually any classroom setting, and give some basics about what is called "brain compatible learning." After that it will outline, over several

---

** Only the author may be held to this guarantee. It should be understood that neither the publisher nor any of the publisher's employees, freelancers, or business partners are obliged to participate in the eating of said sea urchins, nor of any other flora or fauna the author might offer to ingest in the future. If we eat sushi or anything else, we'll do it of our own free will, thank you very much.

chapters, how to use humor in your work successfully, appropriately, and without fear.

(Speaking of fear, Chapter 10 is devoted to the concerns, noted above, that many people have about using humor. If you're really trepidant, you might want to read that chapter first.)

Finally, the appendix offers an example of a teaching module designed with humor, and the bibliography provides a list of resources for further learning.

It is my intent that after reading this book you will:

❖ Feel clear about the benefits humor can bring to the invaluable work you do

❖ Be convinced to start using humor

❖ Have a ready "tool box" of tried-and-true techniques to draw on

❖ Feel fearless about using humor in your classroom (and outside it, too)

So let's not waste any time. With a subject as big as "humor," the question is, where to start? Fortunately, I think I have the answer.

PART I
THE WHAT AND WHY

you've got to start here: what *is* humor, anyway?

A WEALTHY businessman was vacationing on the Riviera, when one day he got a call from home. It was his butler.

"I am very sorry to inform you of this, sir," he said, "but I thought you should know right away. Your beloved cat somehow got onto the roof and fell. I am afraid the animal is deceased."

Expecting grief at this news, the butler was startled at his employer's response: "Hey! *Hey!* Don't they teach you anything in butler school?" Before his servant could reply the man went on: "You don't just *spring* stuff like that on people. You always give bad news by degrees. What you should have done is send me a series of telegrams. The first one says, 'Your cat is on the roof.' Then the next one: 'Cat fallen off roof.' Then another one: 'Cat in critical condition; prognosis poor.' *Then,* when I'm *prepared,* you understand, I get: 'Cat deceased.' See? *That's* how you give someone bad news. Jeez."

The butler, of course, could only apologize profusely and assure his employer this gaffe would never occur again. The businessman tried to put the whole thing out of his mind and enjoy the rest of his holiday as best he could. A week later, just as he was starting to relax once more, he received a telegram. It said:

"Your mother is on the roof."

❖   ❖   ❖

The reason I share the above joke with you (besides the fact that it's my all-time favorite) is that it illustrates the fundamental fact on which this whole book is based: It doesn't work to know the letter of the law and not the spirit. In other words, you can learn all the right moves, but, like the businessman's butler, you can still get it wrong.

Take humor, for instance. People have trouble pinning it down. Indeed, humor seems to be like art—it's hard to define, but you know what you like. Ever hear someone tell a joke, and then hear a listener say, "That's not funny, that's sick"? You just witnessed a clash in definitions. So let's take an important moment to define our terms: What is humor?

The Case Against Teaching Through Stand-Up Comedy

In presenting this topic to thousands of people, I have always started by asking attendees to raise their hands if they think they tell great jokes. In virtually every group (worldwide, by the way), at least 95 percent of the audience sits in resolute stillness. I then ask them to raise their hands if they like to laugh, if they like people who don't take themselves too seriously, if they sometimes wish the whole world would lighten up a little, and so on. Not surprisingly, virtually every hand goes up. Although this hardly constitutes a scientific study, to me it suggests that people instinctively see a difference between humor and joke telling. And there is a difference. Humor is a state or quality. Joke telling is an action—only one of many actions by which you might express humor. In other words (take a deep breath, now): You can use humor beautifully and expertly without telling a single joke.

> "Education's purpose is to replace an empty mind with an open one."
> Malcolm S. Forbes, capitalist

That's right. Joke telling is fine if you like doing it; it is emphatically not necessary for bringing humor into your learning environment or anywhere else. Never tell a joke in your life, and you will still be able to use humor effectively, appropriately, and without fear.

Now, please don't get me wrong: I adore a good joke. Indeed, as you've already seen I use jokes in my own communications. But this is only because I am comfortable doing so. Since I know that most folks aren't, this book will focus on the many other (and in fact, *better*) ways that exist to inspire fun. True, here and there in the book you will find a suggestion to tell a joke; there is even a chapter devoted to the art of telling jokes well. This material is included for that minority of readers who enjoy using this technique. If you are not one of them, do not—I repeat *do not*—bother with it.

Okay, with that out of the way, let's look at the next question: If humor is not joke telling, what is it? It's a state or quality, but of what?

I say humor is openness, optimism—a sort of yes-saying to life. Humor is creativity. Humor is, above all, play. Humor, creativity, and play are the same thing because they all involve the same act: *Finding new connections between things.* This is something everyone needs to be good at. I will prove that now.

The Case for Using Humor in Teaching (and Life in General)

An Irish friend once asked me, "How do you make God laugh?" When I didn't know, he said, "Tell Him your plans." (I don't know what his being Irish has to do with this, except another friend once told me that the simplest humor of the Irish is more profound than the deepest thoughts of the rest of us. Of course, he was Irish, too.) The point here is that life is unpredictable. Life doesn't take requests. Life is like…well, a box of chocolates. (I just made that up. Really.) In this random experiment called Life, we are frequently required to:

1. Make decisions with insufficient data

2. Get the job done with inadequate tools

3. Accept less than 100 percent success

This means that if you're a person who can't live with imperfection, you are in for a rocky ride. You have to be willing to accept—dare I say embrace?—a certain amount of uncertainty. This takes creativity, a.k.a. humor, a.k.a. playfulness.

Look at it this way: If all you can think to do with, say, curtains is to hang them on curtain rods, then what will you do when life hands you just the curtains? Or just the rods? In *Gone With the Wind*, Scarlett O'Hara used a pair of curtains to make a sumptuous gown. That was creative, a new connection; nobody had ever thought of using curtain fabric for clothes. (At least not till the sixties. Say what you will, the sixties were a *creative* decade.) Later, Carol Burnett played Scarlett O'Hara—and wore the dress with the curtain rod sticking out the shoulders. That was humor!

(And when she said, "Oh, I just saw it in the window and couldn't resist," that was great humor.)

Humor, then, is just creativity that doesn't get the expected results. When the unexpected connection works, we call it "creative." When it doesn't, we often find it "funny." Now look at kids. Imagine giving a kid a curtain rod. Would they hang curtains on it? Hardly. They'd make it a rifle. A spear. A light saber. A horse. A high-jump bar. A limbo bar. A baseball bat. A golf

> **"I was wise enough to never grow up while fooling most people into believing I had."**
> Margaret Mead, anthropologist

club. A tent pole. A flag staff. . . .The last thing the little hamster-hugger would *think* to do with a curtain rod is hang curtains on it. That's play.

Kids play with their world in order to make sense of it. A few rare individuals keep on playing after they grow up. These include the likes of Thomas Edison, Grandma Moses, Albert Einstein, Martha Graham, Joseph Campbell, Beatrix Potter—people who have made major contributions to our world.

So. With creativity, humor, and play we seek the unexpected connection, and in the process we discover whole new realms of potential. This means that if you communicate with humor, you will *by definition* communicate creatively and playfully. You will not go for "a laugh a minute," since as you might well imagine, constant, uproarious laughter is not good for learning. Instead, you will play with information and ideas as if they were toys. You will noodle around, see what happens, be ready to be wrong.

Many professional communicators fear this. They think, "I can't *noodle around*—certainly not in front of a roomful of learners! Couldn't I just go into a closet somewhere, be creative from 2 to 4, then send my ideas to some government agency for testing and approval?" And here's the bad news: You can't. First, creativity doesn't schedule well since, again, it isn't an action but a state of mind. Second, if there were a government agency on creativity, the Department of Motor Vehicles would offer free car washes and massages.

Yet today's workplace demands creative thinking skills, as the corporate world continues to reinvent itself. Think about it: The acquisition of information is hardly the challenge today. As Colin Rose, founder and chairman of Accelerated Learning Systems, points out, knowledge is doubling every two to three years—and this is only if you measure "knowledge" by the output of research papers. If you measure it by the amount of data on the Internet, it's doubling—are you ready?—*every fifty-eight days!* And how much of the "knowledge" we receive via the World Wide Web is reliable? How do we know it's true? How do we know where it came from? Meanwhile, even information that can be verified may be obsolete literally within weeks. The knowledge you have today may well be useless tomorrow.

Learning facts is no longer the goal of training and teaching. Learning how to find, assess, and use facts, is the goal. According to Pat Wolfe of Mind Matters, Inc., "Today's 'basic skills' include the ability to think *critically,* and to solve problems in new, unanticipated situations" (read: to think *creatively*).

Humor can be used surprisingly well to encourage critical as well as creative thinking. How do I make this claim? Well, first of all because of the kind of research you'll read about in Chapter 4 and elsewhere. In addition, however, it has long been my observation that people with well-developed minds tend to have a better-developed sense of humor, and vice versa. (Please note that I did not say "well-schooled," but "well-*developed*." I have met more than one person who possesses only a high school diploma—and who has an active, curious mind!) Mentally agile people tend to enjoy and use humor better than most. To me this is no coincidence: The more finely honed one's mind, the better one's discernment of the unexpected connections inherent in humor. Throughout this book, you will see many light-touch techniques that model and cultivate critical thinking about your subject.

> **❝I have never let my schooling interfere with my education.❞**
>
> Mark Twain, author and curmudgeon

Our traditional style of teaching—the Old Learning Model, or OLM—does little enough to develop critical thinking skills. But where the OLM really fails is in teaching learners to think *creatively*. After all, how many teaching professionals today—school teachers, university professors, or trainers—were taught creative thinking when they themselves attended school? Few of us indeed. Yet in a world of constant, rapid change, we all need to teach it now! Teachers and professors need to encourage creativity in tomorrow's workforce. Trainers need to do the same for the workforce of today. Communicators of all kinds need to be able to ignite their listeners' imaginations and open their minds to new ideas. In our disordered, often bewildering era, communicating playfully—creatively—can spell the difference between exciting people about change and reducing them to paralyzed terror.

> **"'Back to basics' teaching doesn't require students to think for themselves, when that is exactly what they will need to do to deal with the increasing complexity of society."**
>
> Colin Rose, Accelerated Learning Systems, Inc.

To teach creative thinking, we have to model it; after all, will our learners take the risk if we ourselves don't? This means we need to shift our own mode of thinking before we can help our learners travel this new road. Fortunately, the ability to think and communicate creatively is inherent in all of us. Don't believe me? All right, I'll prove it. Ask yourself one quick question: Am I a former child?

If you answered "yes," then you're a creative genius! If you don't feel like one, it means you just forgot the rules. You see, as a child you never once stopped whatever game you were playing to say, "Gee, I wonder if I'm playing *right?*" You didn't think, "Hmm, maybe that game wasn't original enough," or "That idea was too crazy" or "That notion is a little rude." You hadn't yet been socialized to think in terms like "right," "crazy," or "rude." You had to be taught those concepts. Someone—most likely your primary caregiver—had to tell you, "Hortense, sweetheart, do *not* play with your saliva," and "Clarence, dear, when Auntie Alice comes for dinner, do *not* ask why she has a mustache." You didn't come out of the gate knowing this stuff!

Of course, our parents and teachers did us all a big favor in helping us learn to regulate our behavior; otherwise we'd never be able to spend twenty minutes in a room together without fights breaking out. But we got one thing wrong: We got that it was somehow "bad" to have rude, crazy, or unoriginal ideas. Yet how can that be? Every idea is just that— an idea. Okay, many of our ideas shouldn't be shared with others, I'll give you that. Most of our ideas shouldn't even be acted upon. But no idea is *per se* bad.

As we have already noted, the world's best thinkers have generally been notoriously playful. They also all had innumerable unworkable—so-called "bad"—ideas. Did you know that Thomas Edison tested no fewer than ten thousand substances to find a light bulb filament that neither burnt out nor blew up? When asked, "you failed *ten thousand*

"I never worked a day in my life—it was all fun."
Thomas Edison, inventor

times?" he replied, "Of course not. I discovered ten thousand things that don't work. Cool, huh?" (Or nineteenth-century words to that effect.) Thomas J. Watson, founder of IBM, said it best: "If you want to succeed, double your rate of failure."

And now for the good news: In Chapter 4, I'll reveal The Professional Comedian's Secret Weapon. This is a technique that takes all the fear out of what comedians call "bombing" (using humor unsuccessfully), and also works beautifully when you publicly share a "bad" idea. On top of that, in Chapter 10 I will reveal the secrets of Noodling Around Without Looking like a Meatball. By the time you finish this book, you will see that it is eminently possible to "fail" in front of others without losing credibility.

Later in the book, you will learn the vital importance of giving the brain "downtime"—a few minutes to process new information. It is for this reason that every chapter contains one or more Reflection Sections, like the one following below. *I strongly suggest you use these as they appear.* You will find your understanding and retention substantially better when you pause to allow the new information you received to incubate. So please take five to ten minutes right now to reflect and write about what you've learned in this chapter.

Reflection Section

Think of your three favorite teachers: Did any of them use humor? How? Which of the kids you knew back in school seem to have the most enjoyable lives today? Why do you think that is? Is it all about high-paying careers, or do they possess a talent for humor, creativity, or play? How do you feel about having "bad" ideas? Should you feel that way? How much of your curriculum teaches facts, and how much teaches *how to think critically and creatively about those facts?*

....

....

....

....

....

....

....

....

....

....

If you're really going to make a change to your time-honored way of teaching, you need to feel confident in your reasons. That's why in

Chapter 3 we'll look at my rationale for claiming that humor is in fact a brain-compatible learning strategy. But first, may I respectfully suggest that you read Chapter 2. That chapter provides a glossary of terms and principles, to which you will continually refer back as you read this book. It has been shown that learners get more out of a program when they are quickly briefed on key concepts and vocabulary in advance. (In fact, this is the reason for the "In This Chapter" notes at the top of this and each chapter—to prep your brain.) So even if you're in a rush to plan tomorrow's program, please read Chapter 2 now. You'll be glad you did.

By the way, it has some really funny material. Does that motivate you just a little more? If so, you now know why I wrote this book. See you on the next page!

come to think
of it, what is brain-
compatible learning?

❖ What Von Restorff discovered about communicating colorfully

❖ The role of states in understanding

❖ Why nonconscious learning is *great* learning!

❖ The four pathways through which the brain receives information

A QUESTION: Can you feel your feet inside your shoes right now?

I'm guessing you probably can. And now for a second question: Were you aware of feeling your feet inside your shoes before I mentioned it? Unless your shoes pinch, probably not. The question is, comfortable or not, why aren't you consciously aware of feeling your shoes at every moment?

The answer, of course, is that you don't have to be.

Consider this: Every organ in your body has a function. Your lungs' function is to take in oxygen and release carbon dioxide; your heart and blood move those and other substances through the body; your liver and kidneys filter out impurities, and so on. In their own way, however, all organs are really doing the same thing: *keeping you alive.*

The brain's function is also to keep you alive. How does it do this? By taking in all the thousands of moment-to-moment bits of information it receives about your environment, quickly analyzing each, and deciding which are important to your survival. The tiny number of bits it codes as "important" are moved to long-term memory. The vast majority ("My pen has black ink," "I heard a car," "This floor is not carpeted") are discarded—and fast, since more bits are coming in each nanosecond.

> **"If we remembered everything, we should be on most occasions as ill off as if we remembered nothing."**
>
> William James, father of American psychology

Undoubtedly you have heard people say that the human brain is like a "sponge." In actual fact, it's much more like a sieve!

This being the case, our job as teachers and trainers is clear: to convince our learners' brains that the information we are conveying is important— that it will *keep them alive.* Unfortunately, we can't just say, "Hey, learn this customer service stuff and you'll live." First of all, that would sound a tad hostile. Second, that's not the process by which brains make that decision. We have to talk to the brain in its own language—to exploit the processes by which it assigns weight to information. This is what *Brain-Compatible Learning* (BCL) is all about.

Let's stop right now and get a basic understanding of BCL. I think you will find as you read that the concept, as well as being fascinating, makes good common sense. Understanding it will further help you to recognize the rationale behind each of the various techniques in this book—and to make sound judgments about any techniques you run across in the future.

❖ ❖ ❖

Start with this fact: We have long known that, absent any teaching strategies at all, people tend to remember what they heard at the beginning and end of any cluster of information, be it a learning module, a speech, a list, a story, or a performance. This phenomenon is known as the Primacy and Recency Effect. The curve of recall looks something like Figure 2-1.

Now ask yourself: Why would the brain decide that beginnings and endings deserve heightened attention? How does this *keep us alive?*

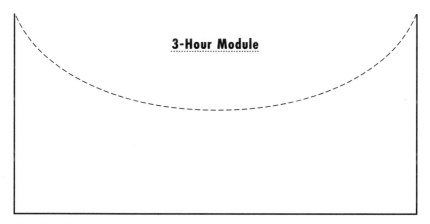

3-Hour Module

FIGURE 2-1. Curve of recall

Could it be that beginnings and endings signal change, something new? Fifteen thousand years ago, we were probably more likely to survive if a change in environment made us sit up and take notice: "Hey, that's a new animal. Never saw one of those before. Can I eat it? Can it eat me?" "Hey, what's that smoke coming out of that mountain? Never seen that happen before. Maybe I should keep an eye on it." After scoping out the unfamiliar situation, we could then relax a bit—until things changed again: "Gee, that member of the opposite sex is staring at me pretty intently. I just swatted her offspring, so it could be bad. On the other hand, I just took that bath—could be good."

Okay, so this is nice to know—that people pay attention to beginnings and endings. It's also the basis of the Adult Learning Model, "Tell them what you're going to tell them, tell them, and tell them what you told them." Notice too that when you signpost throughout a program ("Okay, we've just looked at X; now let's move on to Y"), you are essentially doing mini-summaries and overviews—you are signaling change.

Good to know some of the things you already do are brain compatible, right? But in the meantime, the question becomes: What about the information in the *middle* of your module? Whether your presentation lasts an hour, a day, or several weeks, presumably all of the information is important, and you want your learners' brains to code it that way. And here is where we really go to work: making information too "big" to fit through the "holes" in the "sieve."

For example, if people tend to remember beginnings and endings best, a good strategy might be to create more beginnings and endings. And perhaps not surprisingly, in the 1920s a German researcher named Bluma Zeigarnick found that interrupting a task periodically—even one that was going well—could lead to substantially better recall. The phenomenon came to be known as the "Zeigarnick Effect." The graph now looks like Figure 2-2.

In Chapter 9, you'll learn some fun, quick break activities that you can use in your learning environment. And of course, throughout this book you will find humorous ways to exploit other brain functions—to make

3-Hour Module

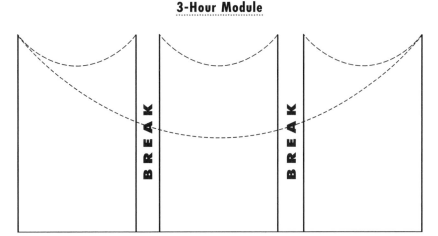

FIGURE 2-2. Zeigarnick Effect

your curriculum points too big to fit through the holes in your learners' sieves. For now, you understand the foundational principle on which BCL is built: that the brain best retains information that it codes as important to your survival, using processes that (in many cases) haven't changed for thousands of years. Next let's look at a few more basic facts about the astonishing human brain. Following is a glossary of some underlying principles of BCL, with insights as to how humor can address them.

Uniqueness

The brain is an astonishingly adaptive organ. It makes connections where it sees they are needed ("Hm, she seems to be doing a lot of mathematical tasks; let's get more dendrite growth over there"), and can even anticipate needed connections ("Yo, newborn baby—we'll need extra language-learning connections till about age ten"). There are also genetic structural differences between sex, age, and other groups. Normal brain development in children can vary from one to three years, which is why in Sweden it is considered acceptable for a child to be unable to read as late as age seven! (Check your emotional response to that one; if you feel a little hit of disapproval you may still have emotional ties to the Old Learning Model. If so, don't worry—you probably just need more proof before you can drop the OLM altogether. That's actually very brainy of you; nice work.)

The point is that since each human being's brain is "wired" uniquely, teachers and trainers must *accept and allow for differences among learners.* Such teachers are flexible and adaptive in their methods; they are creative. And humor, as you saw in Chapter 1, *is* creativity.

Cycles, Rhythms, and Making Meaning

Ever notice that you can't pay attention 100 percent of the time? Ever think it was just you? Well, it's not.

As well as being uniquely wired, our brains also operate, moment to moment, according to their own cycles and rhythms. Cycles are based on our individual Basic Rest Activity Cycles (BRAC—the thing that makes many of us long for a nap in the afternoon), and rhythms on the blood flow alternating between the brain's left and right hemispheres.

These cycles and rhythms vitally impact a person's ability to pay attention. Specifically, they decree when we're in a paying-attention mode and when we're in a reflective, or making-meaning-of-what-we've-just-heard, mode. *In any classroom at any one time, some learners will be in the first mode while most are in the second.* For more on the brain's need to make meaning, see Chapter 9.

Intrinsic Motivation

The brain comes with its own internal reward system—it's actually wired to reward itself! Here's a hypothetical example.

Let's say a colleague told you she'd pay you to wash and detail her car. (Suspend disbelief for a moment, and pretend you wouldn't be insulted.) Brainy person that you are, you'd probably ask, "How much?" Brainy person that she is, she'd probably answer, "How much do you want?" You'd think about things like 1) how much you like (or hate) washing cars, 2) whether you really need the extra cash, 3) what your colleague might be able to afford, 4) what she might be willing to pay, and so on. Finally you'd arrive at the sum—say, fifty dollars. She'd counter, you'd dicker for a bit, and finally you'd agree on a figure—say, thirty-five dollars. You're not thrilled about the money or the task at hand, but you find both acceptable, and agree to do the job. Hey, it's summer; you'll get a tan....

The next Saturday you get out the hose, sponges, soap, and wax, and get ready to go to work. Then it occurs to you: *Your* car could use a wash, too. While you've got all the stuff out, why not do them both?

That day two cars get washed and waxed. One of them—your colleague's—is earning you thirty-five big buckaroos. The other—yours—is paying you nothing. Which car gets the slightly better wash and wax job?

If you said "Mine," you have just seen the difference between the effects of intrinsic and extrinsic motivation. Everyone at least instinctively knows this difference: Extrinsic motivation comes from things outside ourselves, like money, position, or status, and other predictable and/or market-value perks. Intrinsic motivation comes from within. Intrinsic rewards include things like immediate success ("What do you know, I did it"), satisfaction ("I'm always good at tasks like this"), novelty ("Ooh, how interesting"), role model motivation ("I want to do it as well as she did"), and celebration ("Let's hear it for our side"). And intrinsic rewards are the ones that get people most deeply invested in their work.

Well, it turns out fun is intrinsically rewarding! You, I, everyone will always get on board when the task at hand is fun. I guarantee that when you make learning fun, attendees will have to be turned away from your classes rather than cajoled to attend. Even better, they will be more likely to buy in to your material.

The Von Restorff Effect

Throughout history, there have been human beings who could learn huge amounts of information seemingly without effort. In Bombay, for example, the Yogi Shaa could repeat 1,000 phrases perfectly after just one hearing or reading. Professor Aitkin of Edinburgh University could remember the first thousand decimal places of the value of pi. Maori chief Kaumatara could recite the history of his tribe over forty-five generations—a feat that took three days!

Von Restorff was a researcher who studied these so-called memory men. He found that they generally managed their astonishing feats by making information colorful in some way—bizarre, exotic, surprising, frightening. . . or *funny*. Colorful information is memorable because it measurably increases both emotional arousal and attention in the brain.

But wait, there's more! This increased arousal tends to heighten recall of both the colorful information, *and that which comes just before and just after it.* The pattern of recall is shown in Figure 2-3.

Besides accomplishing other brain-based objectives, every technique in this book exploits the Von Restorff Effect by presenting information in colorful (read: humorous) ways.

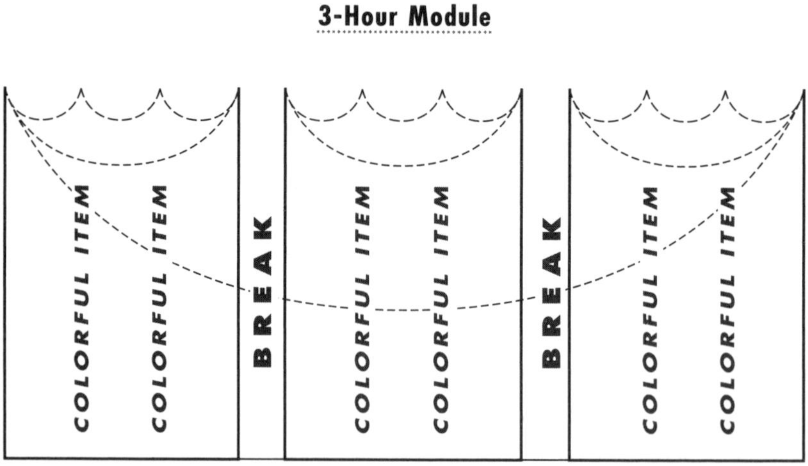

3-Hour Module

FIGURE 2–3. Von Restorff Effect

States

All of our behaviors are dependent on which state we are in from moment to moment. States are not the same as emotions, which you will read about in detail in Chapter 8. Brain-Compatible Learning authority Eric Jensen defines states as "mind-body moments," made up of our beliefs, mental imagery, internal dialogue, and emotions. The seven most common learner states are:

1. *Curiosity/Anticipation:* Curiosity expressed by a tilted head and furrowed brow; anticipation expressed by leaning forward and little blinking.

2. *Disappointment:* Expressed by looking like a blow-up toy that has had some of the air let out: posture slumped horizontally; also, eyes tend to look down.

3. *Fear:* Expressed by a hunched posture or sitting low in chair. The learner seems to be trying to become the smallest possible "target"; eyes are cast down or sometimes glancing about as if seeking the nearest exit.

4. *Apathy/boredom:* Expressed by slumping horizontally, eyes fixed into space.

5. *"Self-convincing" or "I get it!" moment (a.k.a. "knowing they know"):* Expressed by a big inward breath and a shifting of weight, usually in an excited rocking motion.

6. *Confusion:* Expressed by physical asymmetry, like a head tilt; possibly by a hand covering the mouth.

7. *Frustration:* Expressed by more extroverted personalities in pen- or foot-tapping, knee jiggling, pacing, and the like. More introverted personalities will express through tightened jaw, lips, neck, or shoulders.[1]

To best understand states, try acting out physically how *you* behave when you feel the above sensations. Do you slump, lean forward, fidget? What is your face doing? Your breathing? Well, guess what? Other people around the world physically express these states the same way you do! In other words, your learners are constantly and clearly conveying to you which states they are in at any given moment. Cool, huh?

This means you can take moment-to-moment "readings" of your listeners' states, and adjust your delivery to maintain maximum effect. *It is the job of any good communicator not just to be able to read but to manage listener states.* This has nothing to do with "manipulation"—at least no more so than has a good story or movie. You can and should create states of attention, curiosity, confidence, and more, as they are needed. And one of the easiest ways to do this is through the appropriate use of humor.

Nonconscious Learning

In 1957, market researcher James M. Vicary created a popular furor about "subliminal advertising," or advertising designed to be perceived subconsciously by the public. Although Vicary's own "study" was later found to be fraudulent, others followed, ultimately leading the FTC to define a subliminal ad as one "that causes consumers to unconsciously select certain goods or services, or to alter their normal behavior."

Why should this matter to teaching professionals? For one thing, research tells us that the effect of nonconscious communication—unlike that received consciously—continues to increase over time. Even more importantly, research also tells us that about 99 percent of learning is nonconscious!

No professional communicator can afford to ignore this! *At all times, we should be consciously aware of the nonconscious messages we project.* In other words, no matter how clinical, scientific, or technical our topic, we must honor the fact that *how* we present it is at least as important as *what* we are presenting.

As well as through visual imagery, nonconscious learning happens through a speaker's vocal tone, through emotional content. It has been suggested more than once that any serious presenter should take acting lessons, and the idea has great merit. Don't blanch! This could be the most enjoyable skills training you will ever experience! Call your local junior college, or the smaller theatres in your area, and ask about classes, particularly any for nonactors. My own personal recommendation for such training is the wonderful Theatresports,™ a worldwide organization for theatre improvisation.[2] It is not by accident that in this book (as well as in my earlier one, *The Big Book of Humorous Training Games*) I make extensive use of theatre improv games for both you and your learners. Besides benefitting from the creativity training inherent in these games, you will be helped immeasurably to become a better "performer," and thereby a better communicator.

Multipath Learning

Did you know that eyewitness reports are generally considered an extremely untrustworthy form of legal evidence? Why do you suppose that is?

Let's look at another quick analogy for the way the amazing brain works. Imagine yourself entering a bank and proffering a $1,000 check for deposit. The teller says, "Certainly, Ma'am," takes it—and shreds it into a million pieces, which are then scattered throughout the bank. The next week you return and ask to withdraw your money. "You betcha," says the teller—and in a flash, there's your check, reassembled, in your hands. *That's* what your brain does with information. Although certain areas of your brain do specialize in certain types of activities (for example, the left temporal lobe largely handles language, the frontal lobe conscious movement, etc.), generally speaking any information you receive gets "broken up" and sent all over the brain. Is it surprising that when it gets "reassembled," a few fragments of the check are missing? Not at all. Nonetheless, your brain has undeniably performed an extraordinary feat.

You may ask here, why does the brain work in this seemingly inefficient way? But think about it for a moment: All of our experiences are received through the sensory system—vision, hearing, smell, taste, and touch. The same brain cells that are used to store, say, the feeling of softness can be used to recall the softness of a cat's fur, a duckling's down, the pillow on your bed, a baby's cheek, and myriad other things. As Pat Wolfe says, "Our knowledge is built on bits and pieces of many aspects of a given thing. . . but these aspects are not laid down in a single place."[3]

This breaking up of information is in fact a highly efficient way for our brains to organize information.

Back to the case of eyewitnesses. The problem with their testimony is simple: Too many pieces of their "check" can go missing! Retrieval of information is the issue here. All the information—everything they saw and heard—went *into* their brain. The trick is getting it out. They experienced the event when it actually happened, but they must essentially reassemble it every time they retrieve it. After their first "re-collection" of the incident in question, they are merely recalling the recollection. Not too surprisingly, the recollection keeps transmuting. It's kind of like a neural game of "Telephone," except not so innocuous. In fact, for our purposes it can be extremely counterproductive!

So how best to make information retrievable—to enable our learners to get back as much of the "check" as possible? One answer is multipath learning.

Multipath learning refers to the four, well, *pathways* through which information enters the brain: the Semantic, the Episodic, the Procedural, and the Reflexive. Two of these pathways are explicit—carry information easily described or talked about—and two are implicit—carry information we often don't realize we know. Let's look briefly at each.

EXPLICIT PATHWAYS

The *Semantic* pathway receives words, symbols, numbers, and abstractions. You are using this pathway for retrieval when you recite text, recall conversation, describe images, use mathematic formulae, and so on.

The *Episodic* pathway receives events, locations, and circumstances. You use this pathway for retrieval when you answer the question, "Where were you when you heard the Berlin Wall was coming down?" You also use it when you hear the song that was playing on the radio when you learned you were going to be a parent, and suddenly re-experience your feelings, as well as all the sights and smells that were around you, at that moment.

IMPLICIT PATHWAYS

The *Procedural* pathway receives habitual skills; you retrieve through this pathway whenever you ride a bicycle, drive a car, or light up a cigarette after a meal (hmm).

The *Reflexive* pathway receives unconscious information. You use this pathway when you cross your arms (right-over-left or left-over-right?), recoil from the unfamiliar taste of a foreign dish, or grasp the arms of your chair before standing up.

And now for something every communicator must know: *Information that has been received through one pathway is generally harder to retrieve through another.* For optimal retrieval, therefore, you should "send" information through as many pathways as possible. Every technique in this book can fulfill the two brain-based objectives of helping your learners to deposit their "check" securely in the bank (a.k.a., retain information), and withdraw it again with as few missing fragments as possible (a.k.a., retrieve information). In short, you will discover humorous/creative/playful teaching techniques that allow you to send information through multiple pathways at once.

Rhyme, Rhythm, and Music

When I taught traffic school, I got to hear a lot of behind-the-scenes stories from police officers. One thing I learned is that, among other ways of legally establishing that a driver is under the influence of alchohol or drugs, a highway patrol officer will often ask that person to recite the alphabet. This would seem like a simple enough task, but in fact people who are highly intoxicated have serious trouble with it. Apparently it is quite common for these individuals to begin singing, kindergarten-style, "A, B, C, D, E, F, G...H, I, J, K, L-M-N-O-P."

Oh dear. Well, at least they get points for knowing three of the best techniques ever for retrieval of information: rhyme, rhythm, and music.

Think of the rhyming, rhythmic way you learned that "Thirty days hath September, April, June, and November" and "I before E, except after C."

Other examples abound: Flight attendants remember in which direction the plane flies faster with the saying, "East is least." Plumbers and mechanics keep from stripping screws by remembering, "Righty tighty." Add music to the mix, and you've got pure brain food. PET scans show that language is processed largely in the left hemisphere, while music is usually processed in the right. (Note: This is not the same as saying the "left brain" is logical while the "right brain" is creative! The long-popular "left/right" brain theory has in recent years been dismissed as far too simplistic. Still, as brain theories go, "left/right" had a nice, long run. *Vaya Con Dios,* beloved theory!)

In short, when we listen to words and music together, we use more of our brain. In addition, music affects the parts of the brain that process emotion, and as you will see in Chapter 8, emotional learning is powerful learning.

❖   ❖   ❖

As you continue reading this book, start to notice how the above principles of brain-based learning come into play. I will make a point of referring to them, and any new ones that come up, in **bold print**, since Repetition-Repetition-Repetition is yet another brain-based principle.

Speaking of brain-based principles, here's another "Reflection Section." Take a few minutes right now to jot down your thoughts.

Reflection Section

What have you just learned about the brain that makes you want to change what you usually do in your training? Write down everything that comes to mind right now. Don't worry, you can sort through it later. (As you will see in Chapter 4, this is how creative thinking works.) Now is the time for ideas, not fully-developed plans!

....

....

....

....

....

....

....

....

....

You now have a foundational understanding of the principles that will inform your use of humor in teaching. For further reading on brain theory, you can consult the bibliography at the back of this book. For now, let's go to the next step.

As you will see in Chapter 7, the brain most easily retains information that is relevant to it. So we will now look at six excellent reasons to use humor in your work. See you on the next page.

okay, so why use *humor* to deliver brain-compatible learning?

In this chapter:

❖ How humor is both an innate *and* a learned ability

❖ How mirthful laughter affects the chemistry of stress

❖ How humor lets people follow their natural inclinations to feel good and to like each other

❖ How humor and play exploit two big communication tools

❖ How humor can be used to make information "feel real"

❖ How humor and play can help your brain to breathe

THE STORY goes that an Arctic explorer was surveying the vast, icy landscape of the North Pole to get his bearings, when he happened to look over at his native Inuit guide. The man was shivering violently.

"Cold?" inquired the explorer.

"No," replied his companion.

The explorer turned back to his compass and continued to calculate their location. A moment later, he noticed again that his friend was shivering almost uncontrollably.

"Cold?" he repeated.

"Not at all," the man answered serenely.

The explorer looked at him. "Then why are you shivering?" he asked.

His guide gave him a puzzled look in return. "So I won't be cold," he said.

This story nicely parallels why we use humor. Life is full of stress. Many of life's challenges cause us profound discomfort. At these times, our best bet is to react productively. In the case of cold, the most productive response our bodies can come up with is to create internal heat by shivering. Ironically, we look cold to the observer, but in fact we are warming up. We are knocking the problem down to size.

Through humor, we knock other challenges down to size. Psychologist Rollo May says, "Humor is a healthy way of feeling a 'distance' between one's self and the problem." Essentially, he is talking about perspective. It is perspective that best allows us to face our problems squarely—and when we face problems squarely, we make fewer mistakes in solving them. How else can we gain perspective on our problems? Usually through the passage of time. And

> **"Humor is by far the most significant behavior of the human brain."**
> Edward De Bono,
> creativity authority

these days, time is a scarce commodity. This means humor may be one of the cheapest, most effective time-management strategies we can use! Why are we laughing? Ironically enough, so that we can think seriously!

And now let's look at the six main reasons why teachers, trainers, and other communicators should seek to invoke the "foolishness" of laughter in even their most serious communications. The reasons will be briefly outlined below; then in the "How" section of this book, an entire chapter will be devoted to each. Ready? Let's go.

The First and Best Reason: It's Easy and Everyone's Naturally Good at It

Everybody but you, you say? Careful not to confuse humor with stand-up comedy. Remember, it's not your job to be a Joan Rivers or a Rodney Dangerfield. As you saw in Chapter 1, humor is less about jokes than about *play*—and play is an inborn human trait. Edward Norbeck has said: "It seems the more advanced a species is on the evolutionary scale, the more frequent and diverse are its play activities." Both humans and animals play; it seems we

> **"They that are serious in ridiculous things will be ridiculous in serious affairs."**
> Cato the Elder,
> Roman statesman

are "wired" to do so. This fact strongly suggests that play is in some way a survival mechanism. In any event, we are all born with tremendous expertise in it. This brings me to the good news: Repeated experience has shown me that most people can apply their natural playfulness to their learning within the first half hour of any workshop.

When I started out teaching Traffic Violator School, I was extremely nervous. How, I wondered, could I get people who could only be described as "hostile learners" to willingly take part in the Creative Learning I had planned? Within two months, however, that nervousness evaporated. Why? Because I had found that my learners loved to play! Every single group got deeply into the spirit of the thing—not most groups, but *every single one.*

These learners made a 180-degree turn in their attitude toward the class and the learning material. And they did not do it because I stood there telling jokes for six-and-three-quarter hours. (Would you?) No, they did it because they got to use their own, innate playfulness—to reacquaint themselves with one of the best parts of themselves. They had exercised a muscle that, for many of them, had been far too underused for far too long. You could virtually watch their self-esteem rise with their endorphin levels. And it had been astonishingly easy to help make that happen.

Key Point: You may not be able to boost your Intelligence Quotient, but you can certainly boost your Humor Quotient! After that, it's a relatively simple step to help others boost theirs. If this is where you want to start, have a look at Chapter 4.

The Second Reason: It Substantially Reduces Stress and Threat

Sandy Ritz, a disaster response specialist with the University of Hawaii, has a photo of a house badly damaged by Hurricane Andrew. There it stood, leaning at a crazy 45-degree angle; it looked as if the next breath of wind would finish it off. The owners had long since been evacuated. But before leaving their home, they had lovingly spray-painted a message on the garage door. It read: I've fallen, and I can't get up.

It seems we humans have developed a remarkably, brilliantly creative way to confront our fears and relieve our stresses—we laugh! And it's a good thing we do. Brain research shows that threat and high stress seriously impede learning. The brain responds to perceived threat in very predictable ways: The emotional stimulus short-circuits the mental pathways normally engaged in learning, and instead excites the "fight or flight" mechanisms in the mid-brain. Threat and high stress are especially brain-antagonistic in the long run, since the stress hormones released in these states, if chronically present, can literally lead to the death of brain cells! Meanwhile, recent research suggests that mirthful laughing can change the chemical components of the blood, replacing *distress* (negative stress) with *eustress*

> **"Our early emphasis on human relations was not motivated by altruism but by the simple belief that if we respected our people and helped them respect themselves, the company would make the most profit."**
>
> Thomas J. Watson, Jr.,
> founder, IBM

(positive stress). If your learners are highly stressed—maybe just because they don't like being "back in school"—you'll want to make especial use of the humorous techniques in Chapter 5.

The Third Reason: It Draws People Together

Ever been at seemingly impassable loggerheads with another person, when something made you both laugh? Suddenly your differences diminished, didn't they?

Dr. Robert Baron, psychology professor at Rensselaer Polytechnic Institute, tells us people cannot entertain two incompatible feelings—like, say, resentment and amusement—at the same time. As the manufacturer told the client who wanted a high-quality job done both fast *and* cheap: "Pick one and call me back."

When confronted with two conflicting emotions, we pretty much have to do the same—pick one. Again, in my experience, when given a choice between an unpleasant feeling and a pleasant one, we will usually gravitate toward the pleasant feeling. Humor is a pretty impressive phenomenon: Used appropriately, it makes us willing to listen to each other. It makes us appreciate each other more. We just get along better. And as you will see in Chapter 6, this is very good for learning.

The Fourth Reason: It Enlists Two of the Communicator's Best Friends—Relevancy and Visual Memory

I will never forget my first flight on Southwest Airlines. There I was, reading my magazine, serenely ignoring the pre-flight announcement I had heard countless times before, when suddenly came the words:

"Ladies and Gentlemen, there may be fifty ways to leave your lover, but there are only four ways to leave this aircraft."

My head snapped up. I looked to the front of the plane. The flight attendant was smiling pleasantly, pointing out the emergency exits in the time-honored way. I continued to listen, intently now. The announcement went on:

"By the way, there is never any smoking aboard our flights. If we catch you smoking here at Southwest, you'll be asked to step out onto the wing and enjoy our feature presentation, *Gone with the Wind*. Although we never anticipate a change in cabin pressure, should one occur, simply take an oxygen mask and insert a quarter. Unlike President Clinton, you must inhale..."

Southwest Airlines understands something many of us seem to have forgotten: When something is fun, you can't stop people from doing it. Fun is **intrinsically motivating**, and as such, answers the brain's eternal question, "What's in it for me?" The brain has a much easier time holding onto information that answers this question—that feels personally relevant.

See Chap 2

It also has an easier time holding onto information received visually. If I asked you, for example, to memorize the Japanese term for "Good morning"—*Ohayo Gozai Masu*—you would no doubt manage it after a certain amount of repetition. If you created a mental picture from the words, however, perhaps imagining a goat in Ohio with bad eye makeup—"*Ohio goat's eye mess*"—you would probably memorize the term much more quickly. You would also be more likely to recall it years later. (At least I do, fourteen years after taking my single, short-lived course in Conversational Japanese!)

In Chapter 7, you will learn fun ways to make your programs personally relevant to your learners, as well as to exploit visual memory.

The Fifth Reason: It Engages Emotion

Imagine trying to decide where you want to go for dinner based only on a logical weighing of pros and cons. One restaurant has great romantic ambiance, but an unremarkable menu. Another has that mouthwatering duck, but it's all the way across town. Still another has everything you could humanly want in a restaurant—plus prices that scream "Special Occasion." In the end, you must go with a *feeling* about one of the restaurants ("I'd die for some duck tonight!") or you'll never get out the door.

Brain theories come and go, but researchers have long agreed on one point: Without emotion, cognitive thinking is limited.

It is through their emotions that your learners will assign value to your information. Specifically, their emotions will help them decide:

1. How they feel about your topic

2. Whether or not they want to learn it

3. Whether they believe the information they're hearing is true

4. How long they should remember the information

Without an emotional response, your learners may understand your curriculum, but it won't feel "real" to them. In Chapter 8, you'll see in more detail how this constitutes a major problem, and why as much as possible you must deliver your presentations in ways that engage emotion. You will also see how to use humor, creativity, and play in appropriate ways to accomplish this.

The Sixth Reason: It Allows the Brain to Take Regular "Breathers" for Meaning-Making, Heightened Attention, and Review

Remember reading in Chapter 2 about the brain's need to make **meaning** and the **Zeigarnick Effect** (taking breaks to build attention)? There's one more good reason to build time into learning.

In the late nineteenth century, memory researcher Hermann Ebbinghaus found that a learner's typical retention of new information over a given period of time could be plotted on a graph (see Figure 3-1). Ebbinghaus later found that the right amount, spacing, and duration of review could increase recall dramatically. From various experiments in educational psychology, the schedule of review below seems to inspire optimal retention of material. (Note: This schedule assumes a learning module of forty-five minutes' duration):

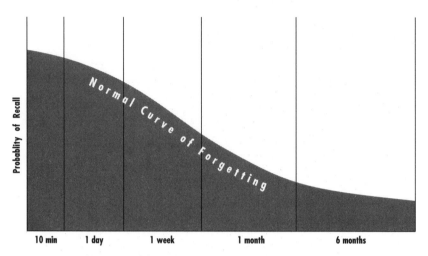

FIGURE 3-1. The curve of forgetting

❖ After ten minutes: Five minutes' review

❖ After one day: Five minutes' review

❖ After one week: Three minutes' review

❖ After one month: Three minutes' review

❖ After six months: Three minutes' review

(Important point: With regard to the first-listed item—five minutes' review after each ten minutes—don't be shocked! Remember that this schedule as a whole suggests an *optimal* scenario. First, we seldom enjoy optimal conditions in life. Second, this 1:2 ratio of review presumes that much of our "check" is "deposited" and "withdrawn" through the **Semantic** pathway [the one that relies heavily on words, numbers, and logic]. Of the four pathways, the Semantic pathway is the only one requiring *conscious intention to remember*. Probably for this reason, it is also the only one employing the strategy of short-term versus long-term memory, that is, quickly dropping information if not coded "important."

See Chap 2

In short, five minutes' review after each ten minutes of curriculum makes sense—*if* you're teaching solely through word, numbers, and logic. Which, hopefully, you're not! It can certainly be argued that, as more and more teaching professionals begin to use Brain-Compatible Learning techniques, the world will come to appreciate the vast amount of learning that happens via the other three pathways. Ebbinghaus, however, was the product of his time, in which linguistic/logical/mathematical was the most—some would say the only—respected intelligence.)

This pattern of review has been shown to increase long-term recall up to 88 percent—a 400 percent improvement over Ebbinghaus' Curve of Forgetting! The improved curve is shown in Figure 3-2.

The key point with all of this is that *the brain can only take in so much information in a given time period.* In other words, holding learners to an intense learning schedule is brain-antagonistic. You must avoid making your curriculum too dense. Loosen up your schedule to give time for exercises, Q&A, reflection, discussion, review, and plain old breaks. This will let your learners interact with the information they've received, to make meaning of what they're hearing—ultimately helping to ensure that their learning will "stick."

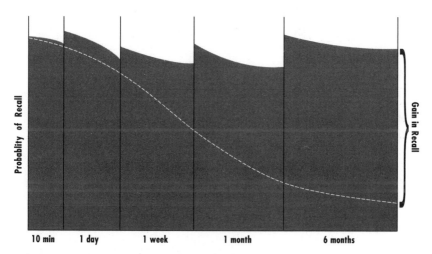

FIGURE 3-2. The curve of forgetting revisited

Many corporate trainers sigh longingly at the thought of a loose schedule. These folks usually work for organizations whose decision-makers cherish two conflicting premises:

1. That their employees need training

2. That they can't be spared from their "real," or "productive" work in order to get the training

Can't the trainer just put the information into some sort of IV drip, these decision-makers seem to ask? Maybe flash the information at the employees while they're eating? Play audiotapes as they sleep?

Although it is true that time is probably the scarcest resource in our world today (next to tolerance, perhaps), the fact remains that anyone who seeks to learn—really learn—needs time. Corporate trainers must accept the fact that a too-dense curriculum looks good only on paper. You tell me which makes more sense: a workshop that presents 100 percent of the information, of which attendees ultimately remember only 22 percent, or one that presents 80 percent of the information, of which attendees retain 88 percent (or 70 percent of the total information)? The indisputable fact is that packing more information into a presentation does not create a better presentation. Making it brain-compatible does.

> **"People who make the worst use of their time are the same ones who complain that there is never enough time."**
> Anonymous

Chapter 9 will show you some light-touch ways to create "pauses" that, when all is said and done, can ultimately yield big savings in time and energy.

Reflection Section

To best enhance your teaching, which of the above things do you need to do most? Build your own HQ? Create better rapport with (or among) your learners? Lower their feelings of threat? Engage more emotion in intellectual or logic-based material? Make your curriculum more personally relevant? Use more visuals? Free up more time for breaks and/or review? Write your thoughts down now.

....

....

....

....

....

....

....

....

....

And now, having clarified the *What* and *Why*, it's time to roll up our sleeves and dig into the *How* of humor. Each chapter in Part 2 will focus on one of the six reasons I've just given for using humor, and suggest specific ways to use humor appropriately in each case. Read on, Fearless One, and learn the first (and most comforting) fact about using humor...

PART II

THE HOW

it's easy—and you can make it easier

five rules for using humor naturally, successfully, and without fear

IN THIS CHAPTER:

- ❖ Why bad ideas are good
- ❖ How being unoriginal can produce amazingly original ideas
- ❖ The ways and why's of positivity
- ❖ How to let your learners help *you* build a Creative Learning environment
- ❖ How to "bomb," and still come out smelling like a rose—Ta-Da!
- ❖ *Lots of exercises!*

IN CHAPTER 1, you read about the need for a workforce that can think creatively. And when do we need that creative workforce? Yesterday! I know that this is hardly news for you. But what may be news is this: As a teaching professional, you have a truly rare opportunity to help translate your organization's mission statement into reality. Again, you will decidedly *not* do so by simply helping your learners to learn facts. You will only do it by helping them learn how to deal with *changing* facts—to think on their feet, remain flexible with new data, problem-solve creatively. To best help them, you yourself will need to model these very abilities. One of the best ways I know to do that is to bring humor into the learning process. So let's get started building your skills!

> **"The illiterate of the twenty-first century will not be those who cannot read and write, but those who cannot learn, unlearn, and relearn."**
>
> Alvin Toffler,
> author and futurist

In Chapter 1, we equated humor with creativity and play. Okay. Hopefully at this point you're pretty clear about the spirit of play. But ways exist to practice the skills—to re-learn what you were born knowing. There are five ironclad rules for being truly humorous, creative, and playful. Following are these rules, along with some games that will let you "get" them at the gut level. Most of the games come from the wonderful world of improvisational theatre, through which thousands of intelligent adults (many of whom never will—and never want to—go onstage) have reacquainted themselves with one of their best qualities.

Many of these games must be played with another person, so grab your spouse and/or kids (the kids'll love it), or a friend or business colleague who is similarly interested in building their humor quotient (HQ), and start having some real, regularly scheduled fun. Play at lunch, in the coffee room, after dinner. (Possibly instead of watching TV? Just a thought.) Definitely bring these games out at parties—they're even more fun than Trivial Pursuit and Pictionary. Then, after you have played them, start using these games (that is, the ones that suit your personal style) with your learners to help them acclimate quickly to Creative Learning.

Rule #1: Cut Yourself—and Others—Some Gosh-Darned Slack!

Why? Because of one fundamental fact which I can absolutely guarantee: Naturally playful and creative genius that you are, most of your ideas will stink.

Yes, it's true. And there is no way around it. If necessary, reread Chapter 1: All of the most creative people have had a hundred lousy ideas before they got to a good one. I can honestly report that in all my years teaching this topic, I have noticed only one difference between creative and so-called uncreative people: Creative people enjoy even their failures. Remember Thomas Edison and his 10,000 attempts to make a light bulb filament? The guy had so much fun solving problems, he didn't see himself as failing!

Here's another, even more compelling reason to cut yourself slack: *If you beat yourself up for having "bad" ideas, you will have FEWER IDEAS, bad or good.*

Remember, your brain is **self-rewarding**: Inside your brain is some- See Chap 2 thing researchers call the Pleasure Center, which effectively lights up when something you do feels good, and makes you want to do more of that thing. Well, think what happens when something you do—like having an unusable idea—feels bad. "Give me an idea, brain. . . . Oh, not *that*, that's too unoriginal. Give me another one. No, not *that*, that's just silly. Another one. No, no, that one's sick! Another. Why, that one's just crazy. . . ." Finally your brain says to itself, "Hey! These idea things are making her feel bad. Enough with the ideas! Let's focus on something that pays off: Let's see, she seems somewhat interested in eye-hand coordination tasks. . . ." Next thing you know, you're threading needles for a living.

Here's a game that will help you—and, later, your learners—learn to cut yourselves some slack:

Trainer Practice: One-Word Instructions

TIME NEEDED

About ten minutes

WHAT TO DO

1. Together with a partner, describe, step-by-step, how to coax a recalcitrant animal to eat. It can be a duck, hippo, baby alligator, anything you wish. The catch—you take turns continuing the sentence, speaking a single word.: "The" "First," "Step," "Is," "To," "Gently," "Hold," "The," "Hippo," "By," "The," "Ears," "And," etc.

2. Keep the pace brisk. As a courtesy, speak clearly and maintain eye contact with each other. Carry on until the animal has been fed.

3. Stop to debrief with your partner: Did either of you ever have to pause to think of a word? That was your Inner Censor blocking you. Rest assured that you had a word, but the Inner Censor insisted on examining it to give (or more likely deny) the stamp of approval. ("Hold the hippo by *what?* Oh, no, I don't think so.")

4. Now play the game again, this time always going with the first word that occurs to you. If it's crazy, unoriginal, or nasty, your partner must (and will) give you a big, warm smile. Then debrief again.

A FEW TIPS

❖ *Keep the pace brisk!* Avoid pauses and um's or ah's.

❖ If you don't hear your partner's word clearly, *don't ask.* Guess what it was, and go with that.

DEBRIEF

❖ What started to happen when you stopped playing it safe and speeded up the pace of the game? What were the positive results? (*Examples:* An increased number of ideas, a greater sense of relaxation, increasing confidence in your ability to come up with ideas spontaneously.) Were there any negative ones? (*Example:* Constantly worrying that you'd blurt out something embarrassing.)

❖ Does the Inner Censor have a place in the creative process? (*Answer:* No. In real life, you'd respectfully invite its opinions only *after* you've finished brainstorming. By the way, this is why you keep the pace brisk—so the Little Dictator doesn't get an opening.)

❖ For the purpose of this game, you gave each other permission to "pop out" with words, knowing that you might blurt out something inappropriate. Would you want to do this with your work group? (*Answer:* Mm, depends. If the group has built up a lot of mutual trust and respect, this will have no adverse effects. But in my experience, this is the rare group. In most cases, inappropriate comments in the workplace are hazardous to your health. So if you play this game with your own work team, you may want to instruct them to keep up the fast pace, but leave out any mention of "going with the first word that occurs to you." [Note: For a full discussion of inappropriate humor, see Chapter 10.] And now congratulate yourself for having had the maturity to play this game in its pure form.)

❖ *Key point:* What might happen if you gave yourself permission to "hotdog" a little more? What might happen if you worked on this skill more often?

Okay, so the "Cut Some Slack" principle helps you to build your own creativity. But does it apply to your learning environment? Yes! Let's look at a few ways.

APPLICATIONS TO THE LEARNING ENVIRONMENT

Besides encouraging and modeling creativity in your learners, this mindset beautifully helps to effectuate the *Aha!*—that magical moment when they "discover," and truly own, content. As you well know, that *Aha!* must come if learning is to stick. But the moment cannot be forced; it can only be allowed. In accepting mistakes and waiting to see what ultimately "shakes down," you actually allow your learners to reach that moment more quickly.

Here's another one: How about that annoying experience all teaching professionals share, in which, after giving clear, careful directions for an activity, they hear a learner ask plaintively:

"What are we supposed to do?"

If you haven't already realized this, it's time you did: *You will never, ever find a way to articulate information so clearly that every single listener will get it the first time.* Maybe they're the ones who "blew it" by not listening; maybe you blew it by not being as clear as you thought you were. Who cares? People blow it all the time—stuff happens. Since you can't change this fact of life, it's high time you lightened up about it. Cut the world some gosh-darned slack!

Learners also "blow it" in other ways. Even in your most fun, intriguing, interactive program, you may find them occasionally walking into the classroom late, leaving early, side talking, and the like. Again, if you cut these folks a little slack, you will often find later that these acts had nothing to do with you or your well-designed curriculum—that those learners had legitimate business to attend to. In the meantime, you will have created a tolerant, learner-friendly environment, in which all of your learners will feel respected, trusted, and empowered.

> **"Learning to ignore things is one of the great paths to inner peace."**
> Robert J. Sawyer, author

In group brainstorming situations, where it's vital for people to feel comfortable "stepping outside the box," Cutting Some Slack is especially important. Here it involves two very specific behaviors:

> **BEHAVIOR 1: Never deride anyone else's idea.**

Why? I promise you, let the members of any group start deriding each other's contributions, and their collective creativity will fizzle out in literally minutes.

> **BEHAVIOR 2: Every member of the group must feel obligated to share even their "bad" ideas with the group.**

Once again, why? Two reasons. First, since you have to go through many unusable ideas to get to the good ones, you may as well do it fast. Get 'em out there! Stink the place up! Dig gleefully through all that manure—somewhere under there, there's a pony! Second, many times an idea that originally seems "bad" turns out to be the winner. Let me give you two real-life examples.

1. A manufacturer of shower heads wanted to create a whole new product market for its product. The brainstorming team reportedly used the creativity game "Random Access," in which they opened a dictionary, pointed to a word, and tried to find all possible connections between the word and their objective. (Remember that creativity involves unexpected connections?) The word they pointed to was "massage." Everyone's brow wrinkled—massage? Little fingers coming out of the shower head? But can you guess the rest? Yes, that's how the ever-so-popular shower massager was born!

2. An R&D group was faced with the problem of inventing a dispenser that could be used with various products from glue to nail polish. The problem was the spout. The thinner substances needed a narrow opening to control the flow. But the thicker substances quickly blocked up the narrow aperture. The engineers realized that what they needed was a self-cleaning spout. As they sat brainstorming one day, one of them reluctantly raised a hand and said, "Ever stood behind a horse as it was answering the call of nature? If so, then you have witnessed one of the most efficient 'self-cleaning spouts' the world has ever seen." Now you, the reader, may or may not have observed the phenomenon to which this engineer was referring and if not, I regret that I will not describe it for you; but as it happened some of the other engineers had.

After the initial groans subsided, one of the engineers suddenly said, "Hey, we could do that!" Needless to say, this company is now the holder of the very lucrative Horse's Patootie Patent. (I made that name up.)[1]

The moral: Share your "bad" ideas proudly! Your contribution may lead to—or even be—the winner. That's how it works.

And now for a common problem that many brainstorming groups share: team members who can't allow themselves to be less-than-brilliant in public. Maybe these people don't believe bad ideas really have value.

"The trouble with the rat race is that even if you win you're still a rat."
Jane Wagner, playwright

Maybe they feel they're on the career fast track, and must protect their professional image. Whatever the reason, the only ideas they offer are those they believe will make them look good.

If this happens within your group, I guarantee a chill will settle over everyone as they realize, "Hey, So-And-So never says anything unless it's smart. Aha, so those are the *real* rules!" (Remember, high achievers often

See
Chap 2

provide strong **role model motivation**.Usually this is a good thing, but in this instance it's not.) Again, the creative process will grind to an abrupt halt.

Here's a ritual I have devised that effectively short-circuits the natural human desire to always look brilliant in front of others. So far, it has worked for me with every kind of group, including training groups.

Presentation Technique: So Sue Me (But I Know You Won't)

WHAT TO DO

1. Before beginning any brainstorming meeting or learning session, explain the importance of "bad" ideas and the two behaviors associated with "Cutting Some Slack": a) Don't deride someone else's idea; and b) share your own bad ideas with the group. Have the group discuss this until you perceive that they have accepted the concept, at least in theory.

2. Now introduce a new team ritual: When anyone has an idea, comment, or question they consider particularly stupid, they must stop everything and announce—*with great pride*—"Hey, I've got a really crappy one here." Whenever this happens, everyone must turn to the Crappy Thought Offerer and express, in any way they choose, their unbridled admiration at the garbage they're about to hear.

3. Have your group practice the new ritual once: On a count of three, have them all say, "Hey, I've got a really crappy one here." (Note: This will get a very healthy little laugh, which you can help along by saying something like, "Wasn't that positively freeing? How often have you thought that very thing, but not said it?") Then, on another count of three, have them all express admiration, however they do that. (Note: The room will ring with spontaneous Ooh's, Ah's, Very nice's, and so on. This will get an even bigger laugh—especially if you express *your* admiration at their natural aptitude with this skill.)

4. Now begin the brainstorming/learning session, with group members offering any and all ideas that occur to them, good or bad.

A TIP

Once the session begins, it works extremely well if *you* are the first one to say, "Hey, I've got a crappy one here!" If the others don't immediately convey their appreciation, stop, look hopeful, and make that little "please applaud" hand gesture. People will remember what they're supposed to do, laugh, and give you your ovation. After that, believe me, they will take this idea and run with it!

In my experience, this simple, two-part ritual takes all the fear out of the creative process for those who are new to it. In addition, it fosters a general atmosphere of congeniality and support. After a time, it may very well become an obsolete custom within your group—it will simply be understood that offering "bad" ideas is not only an act of large-spirited generosity, but also a quick route to success. I should tell you, however,

> **"Creativity is allowing yourself to make mistakes. Art is knowing which ones to keep."**
> **Scott Adams,**
> *The Dilbert Principle*

that I once introduced this ritual to a software company in a single, ninety-minute conference keynote, and two years later found that they were still using it in meetings! What can I say? People just love "So Sue Me."

Reflection Section

When are there times that you don't cut yourself (or others) enough slack? Is it possible that at those times you are "sweating the small stuff"? Do you think this ever puts the brakes on creative thinking and learning? What are some common ways your learners "blow it"? Are they really blowing it? What might you do at these times, rather than play the heavy?

....

....

....

....

....

....

....

....

....

....

And now for the second rule of humor and creativity.

Rule #2: Don't Be Original

This may seem antithetical to my earlier definition of creativity as the act of finding unexpected connections. How, you may ask, can you find those connections if you don't try to be original? But remember the Pleasure Center in your brain? You don't want to turn that little guy off by criticizing all the unoriginal ideas your brain will send you.

> **"It is the essence of genius to make use of the simplest ideas."**
>
> Charles Péguy, French writer

Dare to be boring! Dare to be stupid! Realize that, coming as they do from a born creative genius, even your worst ideas have a spark of divinity in them. Let them come! Ultimately they will lead you somewhere very, very good. . . .

Here's a great game to help you let go of any "originality addiction" you might have. It can be played alone, but is much more fun with someone else.

Trainer Practice: What's in the Box?

TIME NEEDED

Five to ten minutes

WHAT TO DO

1. Picture a 1-foot square cardboard box in front of you. Start to mime pulling things out of the box, rapid-fire. Just make sure they are all original! You may pull out a cobra, a Cajun Ju-Ju doll, a new opera score (sing a little of it), an anti-gravity machine. Pull out as many things as you can, as quickly as you can, before your brain short-circuits. (Don't worry about this somewhat disconcerting phenomenon. In theatre improv we call it "The Brain Fry." Colorful, huh?)
2. Now try pulling things out of the box again, this time making your choices as *unoriginal* as possible: a box of staples, a chocolate bar, a pair of socks, some Kleenex, a bra, another cobra, another Ju-Ju doll, it doesn't matter. Pull as fast as you can until your brain fries.

DEBRIEF

❖ How many things did you get out of the box the first time? The second time? If you're like most people on the planet, you have made my point: We have many more ideas when we do *not* focus on originality!

❖ Were any of your "unoriginal" ideas surprisingly original? If so, second point made. If not, don't worry: It will happen. You can take that to the bank.

❖ *Key Point:* Dig through that manure. Gloves are cheap!

By the way, when you stop trying to be original, you also stop trying to be "funny." This is because your brain has shifted focus from *performance to process.* Now, if you're trying to be a stand-up comic, this is not a good thing. If, however, you're trying to express your natural sense of humor, it is a very good thing! To read further about the importance of not being funny, have a look at Chapter 10. In the meantime.

APPLICATIONS TO THE LEARNING ENVIRONMENT

As you become more adept at the "Don't Be Original" mindset, you will find your brain more readily and joyfully coming up with interesting ways to present training. Maybe you will see ways to better relate content to your learners' interests and personal goals, making it more *relevant.* Maybe you'll get better at writing introductions that "hook" learners into a topic. Almost certainly you'll find yourself delivering curriculum in a style that better engages learners. In short: You will be a trainer who inspires active involvement—just for the fun of it!

Bonus: As time goes on, you'll also become more efficient at sorting the wheat from the chaff—knowing instinctively which of your fun ideas will succeed, and which will not. To use a comedy club term, you'll "bomb" less and less often.

Speaking of "bombing" (a fear I'm sure you have): Yes, all right, sometimes a fun idea you decide to use *will* fall flat on its face. This happens to all fun people in every walk of life—in other words, do not worry about it! Anyway, later in this chapter I will offer the Professional Comedian's Secret Weapon, a technique that takes all the fear out of "bombing." For the moment, just keep the faith....

Reflection Section

Have you ever "stumbled onto" a good idea? What was happening immediately before that moment? Did an unoriginal idea lead you there? What are some unoriginal ideas you have for your training right now? List them all! One of them might get you to the pony....

....

....

....

....

....

....

....

....

And now for the third rule of humor and creativity:

Rule #3: Make Positive Choices

In an experiment on the effects of humor on creativity, subjects were given a comedy video to watch, and then sent individually into small rooms in which they found a cork board on the wall, and on a nearby table a box of birthday candles, a box of matches, and a box of thumbtacks.

They had forty-five minutes to figure out how to affix one of the candles to the cork board in such a way that the candle didn't drip wax onto the floor. While the control groups (who had exercised, or watched films about math) had a 17 percent success rate in solving the problem, the comedy video group enjoyed a success rate of 80 percent![2]

"I've never seen a monu- ment erected to a pessimist."
Paul Harvey, radio personality

A variation of this positivity experiment has been conducted in reverse. Another group of subjects who had been assessed as "nonworriers" was asked to *worry on purpose* for fifteen minutes, and then was given a cognitive task to accomplish. Their ability, previously measured in such tasks, deteriorated sharply.[3]

At this point it seems undisputable that thinking improves dramatically when our mindset is positive. Thoughts of happiness, beauty, love, or nobility seem to create more mental agility than do those of sadness, loss, revenge, conflict, and so on. In short, it seems that the mental state of the truly creative soul must always be one of "YES!"

Sound like more than you can manage in these times of constant change and high stress? I will now offer a two-person game to illustrate the point.

(That is, I will do so as soon as I tell you how to affix a candle to a corkboard so that it doesn't drip wax on the floor—otherwise part of your mind will remain back on this problem, and you'll have less attention to give to the subjects at hand. So here you go: You empty the box of thumbtacks, tack the box to the wall by its lid, light a candle, drip a little wax onto the floor of the box, settle the candle into the wax, and voilà! Happy? Good. Now let's look at the game.)

Trainer Practice: *"Fortunately..."*

This game involves what comedians call "turn-about" humor: finding reasons that good things are bad, and bad things are good. This is far easier than it may sound. Few blessings in life are unmixed; seldom do we find a cloud without a silver lining, or a silver lining without a cloud. Traditionally, comedians have focused on the *cloud:* "I slept like a baby last night—I woke up every hour and cried." "You look like a million bucks— green and wrinkled." "Your teeth are like stars—they come out at night."

Interestingly enough, newer generations of comedians have turned this tradition on its ear by focusing on the silver lining. Bill Murray is one example. In the movie "What About Bob?" a boy tells about falling into the lake and having his whole life flash before his eyes. Bill Murray's character answers, "You're lucky you're only twelve!" That's the kind of thing I want you to do here: focus on the silver lining.

TIME NEEDED

Approximately ten minutes

MATERIALS NEEDED

Some negative statements written on slips of paper. Each statement should focus on just *one* negative thing—no compound tragedies, please! Here are enough to start you off (life being what it is, I'm sure you can easily come up with more on your own if you need them):

❖ *Surprise, you're having triplets!*

❖ *Yep, that tooth will have to come out.*

❖ *Your computer just crashed—again.*

❖ *I'm afraid your credit card was refused.*

❖ *Your house has termites.*

❖ *Looks like our flight to Tahiti has been cancelled.*

❖ *Um, there's a boa constrictor in the crawlspace.*

❖ *You got fifty e-mails today. I think about half of them are Internet jokes.*

WHAT TO DO

1. With your partner, determine who has the shiniest shoes. That person is Partner A.

2. Person A starts by pulling a negative statement out of a hat, and reading it to Partner B. Partner B must then respond, "Fortunately," or "Great!" or "Yay!" and complete the sentence any way they wish. Two rules: They may neither gainsay the statement—"That's not true"—nor simply claim to be happy about the negative thing. Instead, they must find a reason *why* the negative thing is actually good. *Example:* "You got fifty emails today. I think about half of them are Internet jokes." "Cool! I can delete those twenty-five, and cut my reading in half!"

3. Switch off: Person B now reads a negative statement, and lets Person A say why it's so fortunate.

4. Continue until all the negative statements have been turned around.

DEBRIEF

❖ For many people, it's easier to turn positive things into negative ones than the other way around. Why might this be? [Note: Psychologist and author Martin Seligman suggests a possible reason for our apparent preference for negativity. Our most recent evolutionary ancestors lived during the Pleistocene Age, a time of great climactic catastrophes. The ones most likely to survive that difficult era were probably those with solid skills in pessimism— who saw every sunny day as an anomaly, and so remained better prepared for the hard times they were sure would follow. In other words, *we may all be the descendants of worry warts!*[4] This is just another example of the how little the brain has evolved over the past few (or actually, many) thousand years. The good news is, with a little practice we can rewire our brains in this respect. Many have done so, and you can, too. Think of yourself as a sort of evolutionary pioneer, leaving a new legacy to your own descendants!]

❖ What if your work team was given an impossibly tight deadline on a project, and you said in a bright tone: "Wow, this will be character-building"? Would it get a laugh? Might it be a *different kind of laugh* than that inspired by a negative joke? In what way or ways?

APPLICATIONS TO THE LEARNING ENVIRONMENT

The "Positive Choices" principle extends also to your habitual *verbiage*. The words "This material is not difficult" do not mean the same to your learners as "this material is easy." The second statement is essentially an **affirmation**. Brain research suggests affirmations have a powerful and lasting nonconscious effect. Key Point: Replace negative verbiage with positive wherever you find it!

See
Chap 5

In brainstorming sessions and classroom discussions, the "Positive Choices" principle extends further to include simple, habitual *agreement*. By this I do not suggest that you should go along with all ideas—yours or anyone else's— but only that even if you don't at first instinctively like an idea, you should stay with it for at least a few moments. Remember that in the idea-generation/absorption stage, nothing is yet

"Where there is an open mind, there will always be a frontier."

Charles F. Kettering, inventor

carved in stone. No harm can come from a delightful attitude of agreement on your part, except more ideas, since you create a safe atmosphere of openness and exploration. In addition, you will inspire a greater attitude of agreement on your partner's part toward your own ideas.

Bottom line: Actively seek reasons why *everyone's* contribution might be wonderful. You could be right!

Here's a two-person game that will illuminate the value of agreement:

Trainer Practice: Yes *but*—Yes *and*

TIME NEEDED

Five to ten minutes

WHAT TO DO

1. With your partner, look to see who has darker (or if it is the same color, longer) hair. This is Person A.

2. Start planning a dream vacation, with each person speaking only one sentence at a time. Person A starts: "Let's go to the lake (the mountains, Hawaii, or whatever) for our vacation." Person B rejoins, "Yes, *but*—" and finishes the sentence any way they want: "Only if it's not too crowded," or "Can we drive there?" or "Let's be sure to take lots of sunscreen." Person A always answers: "Sure!" then adds another idea: "We could rent a houseboat." Person B again says, "Yes, but," and adds their bit, like, "it can't be a big one," or "how will we sleep with all that rocking?" or "I want a maid; I'm not doing all the cleaning like last year," or whatever. Person says, "Sure!" and adds something else. And so on. Keep this up for one minute, then stop.

3. Now try it again, with one difference: When A makes a suggestion like: "Let's go to Paris for our vacation," B replies with "Yes, *and*," and then adds something: "let's visit the Louvre," or "let's study French to prepare." Keep it up for one minute.

DEBRIEF

❖ *Person A:* Did you have more fun playing this game in Round 1 or Round 2? What was the experiential difference between the two rounds?

❖ Compare the two vacations you just ended up with. Which one was more interesting? Which was more fun to plan?

❖ In real life, how does a "Yes *and*" attitude affect thought and interaction? How about a "Yes *but*" attitude?

❖ Is a "Yes but" attitude needed sometimes? When?

Key Point: You will create more momentum—and be more fun to work with—when you build on your partner's ideas instead of tearing them down. Become as much fun as you can as quickly as you can: Try another two-person game now.

Trainer Practice: Supply the Word

TIME NEEDED

Ten to fifteen minutes

WHAT TO DO

1. Look at your partner and decide who has the more interesting watch. That will be Person A.

2. Come up with a title of a story that's never been told—for example, "The Salami Sandwich."

3. Person A begins telling the story: "Once upon a time there was a _____ ." Person B now fills in the noun, like: "guy."

Person A: "His name was _____ ."

Person B: "Ralph."

Person A: One day he ate _____ ."

Person B: "A salami sandwich."

Person A: "It tasted _____ ."

Person B: "Great."

Person A: "And made him _____ ."

Person B: "Thirsty for a soda."

And so it goes: Person A creates the situation, while Person B identifies the specifics. Continue until the story feels as if it's reached the end.

DEBRIEF

Be honest: While playing this game, did you ever think, "No, don't say *that*—I wanted you to say *this*"? This gives you a good idea why we so seldom say "yes" in life: We're married to our own ideas. Which doesn't mean they aren't good. But in this game did you at least once have the experience of letting go of your idea—and with your partner finding a better one? If not, then play the game again! You need to know that that happens.

Reflection Section

Think about the negative things that happen in your workplace. Think about a mistake you, or one your learners (or even your corporate decision-makers) have made. Can you find the silver lining? Write down some examples. (Tip: I'll be asking you to use these later.) Important question: Does your own humor ever tend to be negative, sarcastic, or derogatory in nature? If so, what effect do you think that has on others around you?

And now for the fourth rule of humor and creativity:

Rule #4: Focus Out, Not In

Probably the best joke I ever wrote was about the wedding of Prince Charles and Lady Diana Spencer. It was also delivered in the Vancouver comedy club, Punchlines, the night before that wedding. (This is called "timeliness"; everyone was sick of the endless news coverage of the Royal

Wedding, and I was likely to get a good laugh by playing off this fact.) In the role of a newscaster for the BBC, I read the following "story" in my best English accent:

> A previously unknown disease is sweeping Southern England, where it is reported to have reached epidemic proportions. Doctors are baffled by a strange malady whose only apparent symptoms are prolonged vomiting followed by death. Although medical researchers have not yet determined the cause of the disease, in honor of the Royal Wedding they've given it the name "Chuck and Die."

This got the kind of laugh every comedian lives for: Guffaws-with-Applause. Needless to say, I was tremendously satisfied with myself that night.

A couple of weeks later I was at another club doing a different bit: a Bette Davis impersonation. At one point in the act, "Bette" announced that she was about to do impressions of other stars. The gag was to be that all of her impressions—John Wayne, James Cagney, etc.— still sounded completely like Bette. (Are you wishing regretfully that you had caught one of my performances back in those glory days? I can well imagine your sense of loss. Try to be strong. . . .) In character, then, I began: "Many people think of me as an award-winning actress, a glamorous movie star, a film icon. But did you know that I also do brilliant celebrity impersonations?"

I got no further. A heckler in the front row immediately called out: "Impersonate *Bette!*"

We may accurately describe what ensued as Prolonged Guffaws-with-Applause. The audience howled. They clapped till their hands blistered. As comedians like to say, they died.

As it happened, I did, too—let's face it, that was a funny line. The fact that I laughed as hard as everyone else probably got the audience onto my side. Then, when we had all settled down, I moved back up to the mike. Still in the role of Bette, I said the first thing that came into my head. As it happens, it was a comment a friend of mine often used when I gave her a hard time about anything:

"You doggie lips."

The audience howled. They clapped. They stomped. They cheered. They raised the gosh-darned roof. Weeks later, someone came up to me on the street and said, "Doggie lips—I thought I'd wet myself. Where'd you *get* that?" Meanwhile, I wandered around in a state of pure bewilderment. Here I sweat blood writing and rehearsing something that is actually funny, I thought, and I get a good laugh. Then I pop out with something luke-warm at best, and I practically get offered the keys to the city. What on earth is this comedy thing all about?

Again and again over the following months, I witnessed the same phe-nomenon. Almost always, the most mediocre interaction between a come-dian and their audience got laughs as big as did their best-written jokes. Then one day I got it: *In the former instance, the audience was part of the act!* At any moment it could be their turn! There was the excitement of immediacy; anything could happen! Not long afterward, I left the world of stand-up for good, and began doing theatre improvisation instead; that interactive stuff was just *way* too much fun to ignore. But I never for-got the lesson, and when I began teaching I knew it was just as true in the learning environment as it had been on the stage. The fact is, our learners don't *want* us to be the Purveyors of All That Is Great in our learning environments—they want a hand in it, too! They want the See Chap 2 **intrinsic motivations** of recognition, appreciation, and feedback. They want attention focused on *them*. And that's exactly where our attention should be focused—outward, on them.

Focusing *in* means listening to yourself, watching yourself, constantly gauging your effect on others. Focusing *out* involves listening and responding to *other* people's quips and cleverness. The communicator who focuses inward will often speak at long length, and then when a lis-tener offers a comment, simply say, "M-hm, yes," and carry on as before.

The communicator who focuses outward will create a "stop" at each instance of listener input, *yes-anding* them, so to speak, incorporating their offering into the discussion, taking pains to show that the listener has contributed and the leader appreciates. If there is nothing much to say in response to a learner's remark, these speakers still acknowledge it with energy: "Yes!"; "Exactly, very nice"; "Great"; "Absolutely"; "Thank you"; and so on. What they don't do is let the comment lie there like a limp carrot.

The communicator who focuses out creates an environment in which anyone can be part of the show, and anything could happen. This keeps people awake; you may take that to the bank.

By the way, those three words—"anything could happen"—fill many professional communicators with dread. What if an attendee, encouraged by all your personal attention and encouragement of spontaneity, becomes, how-you-say, highly verbal? Has an agenda and tries to take over? Or, worst case scenario, just blurts out something in truly bad taste? Isn't this too high a risk to take for the "excitement of immediacy"?

First of all, let us bow our heads and acknowledge that these dangers exist in any gathering of human beings. Next let's remember that in Chapter 10 you're going to learn techniques for "Noodling Around Without Looking Like a Meatball." For now, however, it behooves us to practice Focusing Out, Not In. Since you'll obviously need someone to focus out on, the following games are played in groups, and work best when there are between six and twelve people. These games should be played with your peers first, but can also be useful when played with your learners, since they illustrate the value of listening and collaboration.

Trainer Practice: Go

WHAT TO DO

1. Have your group stand in a circle.

2. One person starts things off: Making eye contact with another member, they loudly say, "Go!" then quickly walk toward that

person, taking their place in the circle.

3. The second person must now move. Looking at someone else, they say, "Go!" and walk across to take that person's place. The third person does the same with a fourth, and so on.

4. Keep things moving fast, and after awhile, speed it up: Don't wait for your "Go-er" to begin walking toward you; with just the word and the eye contact, immediately look at another player, say, "Go!" and head for them. Get to the point where there is always more than one person moving at any one time.

5. Finally, eliminate the word "Go" altogether—just make eye contact and *move!* See how many people can be moving at once while still knowing at every point whose "turn" it is.

DEBRIEF

❖ In what ways did we have to focus outward to make this game work well? [*Answers:* Made solid eye contact; checked to ensure our partners "received" our signals; took care of each other, so to speak.

❖ *Key Point:* Could we have moved at optimal speed *without* these techniques?

The above game allows you to see how much more quickly we "pick up" on other people's signals than we think, as long as we focus out. It also shows how much pleasure we human beings derive from doing so. Here's a game that illustrates these things even better, and one that I think will intrigue you as it always does me:

Trainer Practice: Group Count
WHAT TO DO

1. Have your group sit in a circle, close their eyes, and count to twenty, with only one person speaking at a time. The order of speakers is completely random: One person may speak more

than once, another not at all. The tempo may speed up or slow down as you wish. There is no signaling whose turn it is to speak—but if two people speak at once, the group must start counting again from 1. That's it.

2. Go until the group reaches twenty (don't worry, sooner or later they will), then pause to debrief.

3. Inform everyone that the object of game is *not* about finally getting to twenty! After all, if it were, the game would be insultingly easy: The group would simply use a signal, like tapping a finger or clearing a throat, before each member spoke. Then, of course, the game would be over in a flash (and, incidentally, no fun). In actual fact, the object of this game is to *know whose turn it is to speak.*

4. Tell them that you're going to try it again, and that this time each person must wait till they somehow get a strong "hit"—a sense of complete certainty— that it's their turn to supply a number. If they get that "hit," they should speak up at once. If they never get the "hit," fine—their turn will come the next time you play the game.

5. Now try counting again, this time not worrying about achieving the illustrious goal. Just listen to the "message in the silence." See how long it takes you to get to twenty this time.

DEBRIEF

❖ What happened when we waited for the "hit"? Did it make a difference?

❖ How often do we speak up without listening—without getting that "hit"? Do we ever speak only to fill the silence? Is there a "message in the silence"?

In some strange way—don't ask me how—every single group I've ever played this with has gotten to twenty much faster when they use the second technique of waiting for the "hit." Of course, until you play this game for yourself you'll only have my word on that. So give it a try! Play as often as you like. Once your group has reached twenty with ease, make the goal twenty-five. Then thirty. Enjoy!

APPLICATIONS TO THE LEARNING ENVIRONMENT

Probably the most valuable thing the "Focus Out" principle will bring into your work is a more *genuine responsiveness to your learners*—a habit of *Yes, And*-ing their comments rather than just giving a noncommittal, "Mm-hm," or "I see," or a facetious "Yeah, great" (or the dreaded, "Yes, but. . ."").

A tip: One very easy way to "Yes, *and*" is to simply rephrase what someone has said. For example, if they said, "I was confused by this exercise," you might respond, "Didn't make sense to you, huh?" While this doesn't actually add any new information to their comment, it does send the message that it interested you enough to interact with it.

Focusing out will also encourage you to design programs that are not too information-dense. How, you ask? One reason is that you will want to allow enough time for your learners to ask **questions**, an act that is vital to long-term learning. You will also want to employ **peer feedback**, another highly effective strategy. Make discussion groups a part of your learning format. Invite learners to answer each other's questions, or to act as "Guest Experts," addressing the class when they happen to have specialized knowledge about a subject you are covering, or when they've had an experience that illustrates something the group is learning.

See Chap 10 & Chap 6

"To teach is to learn twice."
Joseph Joubert, eighteen-century French philosopher

Best of all, create learner teams and let them present subsections of the curriculum (much more on this in Chapters 6 and 9). All of these techniques allow you to share the stage while promoting better learning—and all of them require a program with built-in "breathing space." Remember what I said in Chapter 2: Dense curricula look good only on paper.

And now for the most important way to focus out: *Be their biggest fan!* Exhibit as much (if not more) interest in their contributions as in your own. Always laugh at their jokes, as long as they are not inappropriate

(Chapter 10). Make a point of mentioning a learner who had a useful question or comment at break. Do anything you can think of to transfer ownership of the learning process to its rightful owners—your learners.

The story goes that a woman dined with the two greatest statesmen of Victorian England, William Gladstone and Benjamin Disraeli, on two consecutive nights. Asked for her impressions of these two people, she said: "When I left the dining room after sitting next to Mr. Gladstone, I thought he was the cleverest man in England. After sitting next to Mr. Disraeli, I thought *I* was the cleverest *woman* in England." Think about it: Which man would you rather have had dinner with?

> **"The greatest good you can do for another is not just to share your riches but to reveal to him his own."**
> Benjamin Disraeli,
> Victorian statesman

Reflection Section

How do you feel about people who make you laugh—but never give you a chance to do the same for them? What about teachers who tell, but never ask? At what moments in your training do you think you're most focused on yourself? Which of the above techniques can you use to change that? How else might you design your training to be more outwardly focused?

....

....

....

....

....

....

....

....

And now it's time to look at the fifth (and *extremely* important) rule of humor and creativity.

Rule #5: Always Acknowledge the "Bomb"!

This rule is based on a fact of which by now you are very well aware—that as a born creative genius, most of your ideas will stink. Put in a stand-up comic's terms, you will "bomb."

As a former stand-up comic, I am an expert in the subject of bombing, and so you should listen to me: YOU WILL BOMB! In fact, you'd better; if not, you're not trying anything new, which means you're not being creative. The irrefutable reality is that everybody—Robin Williams, Julie Brown, Billy Connolly, pick your own favorite—has bombed, and will bomb again. Unlike most of us, however, these professionals know that it's perfectly okay to bomb! You just need to have the Professional Comedian's Secret Weapon, which I will now reveal. Ready? (I could get drummed out of the corps for this, but here goes:)

> **PROFESSIONAL COMEDIAN'S SECRET WEAPON**
> **Be the first to point out that you just stunk the place up, using a humorous "ad lib" you made up in advance.**

You read right: A humorous "ad lib" you *made up in advance.*

In case you weren't aware of this, every comedian has a ready store of so-called ad libs, just in case they bomb. I believe it was Jerry Lewis who said, "My best ad lib took about seven hours to write." Political speech-writers never ignore this vital necessity. In 1988, then-vice president George Bush made a (Freudian?) slip during a campaign speech. He said, "We've had triumphs. We've made mistakes. We've had sex." He'd meant to say "setbacks." After the audience had picked itself up from the floor, Bush observed, "I feel like the javelin thrower who won the toss and elected to receive." On the Nightly News, Connie Chung reported his gaffe—and his excellent "recovery."

Bombing, and then humorously acknowledging your bomb, can give your listeners three wonderful gifts:

1. Freedom from having to feel embarrassed for you.

2. Renewed respect for your competence and confidence. (After all, you were smart enough to know that you just bombed, and confident enough to put it into perspective.)

3. Reassurance that they themselves might bomb in front of you without fear of ridicule. (Note: This one is no small gift!)

To sum it up, far from harming your credibility, a nice little bomb can actually *increase* rapport and trust between you and your listeners. Makes you want to go right out and bomb like there's no tomorrow, doesn't it?

Okay, don't get too excited. Before embracing this technique, it is imperative that you know the difference between a "bomb" and a "mistake." A mistake is something that causes actual damage or injury, puts someone in danger, or embarrasses them. A bomb is a harmless gaffe that causes only embarrassment—and only to you. To ensure your understanding of this important distinction, take a few minutes now to take this quick self-test:

QUICK SELF-TEST: WHICH ONE IS THE BOMB?

1. Losing a million dollars of your company's money

2. Accidentally deleting the payroll files

3. Totaling someone else's car

4. Breaking your partner's foot on the dance floor

5. Letting your beloved mutt get loose and mate with the neighbors' prize-winning Corgi

6. Tripping over your wedding dress and falling on your bouquet

7. Tripping over your wedding dress and falling on the flower girl

---

If you checked number 6, congratulations—you're clear on the concept of bombing!

We should always apologize for our mistakes, but never for our bombs. Think about it: How many people go into some kind of *mea culpa* song and dance every time they bomb: "Oh, I don't know why I tell jokes, I'm just terrible at it"? What are these people really doing but asking all those present to interrupt their busy lives in order to watch another human being writhe in self-loathing? Mmmm, *fun!*

So will you now please raise your right hand and repeat after me: "For the comfort of myself and others, and in the interest of world creativity, I will always acknowledge the bomb." Come up with your own ad libs: "Thank you, ladies and gentlemen, I'll be here all week!" or "That moment was just for me, and I must say I enjoyed it." Even stopping dead and saying, "Thank you, thank you very much" will do the trick. Say or do *something.* But do not—do *not*—pretend it never happened.

And now I ask you to notice something. The three "ad libs" I just listed are all positive in nature. This was no accident. Yes, George Bush got a good response from what was essentially a negative ad lib, and you can, too. But I have found that positive ad libs consistently get a better response. Picture this: You've just laid the biggest egg of your life in front of a whole roomful of peers. They are all looking at you with a mixture of bland amazement and pity. You look back at them and smile.

Then you use ad lib #1: "I'll just go clean out my desk now."

Or, alternately, you use ad lib #2: "I'll take that corner office now."

I virtually guarantee that both lines will get laughs. But can you see that ad lib #2 will get a bigger one? More importantly, can you feel the difference in the quality of laughter it will evoke? We have already examined the value of making positive choices. In my experience, *positive ad libs work best in humorously acknowledging a bomb.*

There is a joke about a guy who wanted to be a magician. He practiced his craft day and night, and finally got his first break as an opening act in the Catskills. Bringing an audience member onto the stage, he handed her a mallet and instructed her to hit him over the head as hard as she could. Though understandably reluctant, she was at last prevailed upon to do so. And, as might be expected, he dropped like the proverbial stone. An ambulance was called. He was taken to Emergency, and from there to Intensive Care, where for twenty-five long years he lay in a dead coma. One night a nurse, passing by his room, noticed a slight sound. Bolting in, she was just in time to see him open his eyes. They fluttered, rolled a bit, and then focused on her. A smile touched his lips.

"Ta-Da!" he croaked.

Ever see a circus clown? They trip, they fall down, they get kicked in the pants and have seltzer sprayed in their faces. And what do they always do? Jump up, throw their arms into the air and mime a grand "Ta-Da!" And what does the audience do? Applauds. The psychological dynamics here are fascinating. Watching someone experience misfortune—even staged misfortune—creates distress. When that person rebounds with the laugh of a fool, we are allowed to vent that distress with our own laughter. This is why slapstick (which personally I've never much enjoyed) continues to get big laughs (sometimes even from me). As well as venting our stress, such "low brow" humor also reminds us of an essential truth: Most of life's calamities are only as bad as we make them.

Serve up this beatific truth to others as often as possible. You needn't leap about or wave your arms like a clown. Just chuckle at the unexpected. Nod with wry amusement at your own *faux pas*. Smile with delight at the hidden logic in another's mistake. **"Bombing is what gets you good."** You know life can be weird, irrational, and inconsistent; remind others of that fact, along — *David Brenner, comedian* with the priceless addendum that it's often no big thing. Share the eternal wisdom of the bumper sticker: "Stuff Happens." (Okay, so it doesn't say *stuff*, but let that be.) Or say with the British, "Let's not get our knickers in a twist." Or just bow. It makes people feel good.

Hey, I've got an idea—why don't you try it right now?

Trainer Practice: The Clown Bow

WHAT TO DO

1. Stand up, wherever you are, fling your arms out and say, "Ta-Da!"

2. Look around to see if anyone is staring. Smile at them. Sit down.

3. *Alternative:* Do it in secret.

4. *Key Point:* Just do it. It won't kill you.

This activity speaks to the central concept in this book better than any other, and is therefore the most important of all. So you really should do it, no matter how silly it may appear to you now. To be a truly creative, humorous learning professional you will need to feel—really feel—completely unembarrassed by any bomb. The physical act of doing the Clown Bow will allow your brain to start making the concept "real," even if you don't yet quite believe that bombing is okay. Get this all-important concept into your bones. Once you have, then polish your act. Write (or steal, the *real* Comedian's Secret Weapon) your own personal "ad libs." Use any of those listed above, or get some from a sitcom, the funnies, a comedy club. Whenever you use your ad libs in the future, do so in the spirit of the Clown. Ta-Da!

Reflection Section

What concerns do you have about using the *Ta-Da* in real life? Have you ever witnessed people who used the *Ta-Da* naturally and comfortably? What was your general impression of these people? Have you known others who habitually sought to cover up their "bombs"? What was your impression of them?

....

....

....

....

....

....

....

Some Next Steps

1. Get a "playmate," and schedule some regular playtimes for the next month. Commit to these—they can pay off BIG over the long term!

2. Look at the "silver lining" examples you listed in the second Reflection Section in this chapter. Use these kinds of positive, turn-about observations as your sole form of humor for the next week. Observe the response.

3. Stage a Friday or Saturday night potluck party at your house, and play "One-Word Instructions," "What's in the Box?," "Gibberish and Interpreter," "Yes but/Yes and," "Supply the word," "Go," or "Group Count."

4. Suggest "So Sue Me" at your next problem-solving meeting. Be the first one to say, "I've got a really crappy one"—then look expectant until they applaud.

5. Go over one of your written communications—maybe a letter, memo, or speech you're writing—and rephrase as many negative statements as you can into positive ones. Example: "This

will not take place before the 8th" becomes "This *will* take place on or after the 8th."

6. Make a vow to Clown Bow your way through your next bomb (which, if you're a normal person, should take place within the next twenty-four hours).

7. Start stealing ad libs.

You've just looked at techniques for cultivating your natural talent with humor and creativity. These techniques will give you a solid start down the road to delivering your message in ways that 1) more deeply engage your listeners, 2) help them remember your curriculum, and 3) encourage them to think creatively about it. Any communicator has got to like that!

By the way, there is one final, immensely important secret to becoming more humorous, creative, and playful. But I am saving it, to be discussed at length in a specially-reserved chapter—that's how important it is. To which chapter do I refer? Here's a hint: It's the best one in the book. But I've already said too much; spies are everywhere, and I must flee. Courage, Fearless One. When next we meet (specifically, on the next page), I will reveal how, newly comfortable with your innate creativity, you can use humor to accomplish the initial Brain-Compatible Learning imperative...

> **"If you use joke telling as your only form of humor, please don't tell people you read this book."**
>
> Doni Tamblyn,
> recovering stand-up comedian

deposing the brain's great oppressors

threat and high stress

FOLLOWING IS a true story about my eighth-grade math teacher, Mr. D. I will never forget him: Mr. D was a big guy (he also taught PE) with a military-style haircut and a no-nonsense attitude. His first-day speech went something like this:

> You will not be late to this class. If you are late three times, you will get...THE STRAP! *(Illustrated by whacking the actual implement of correction on his desk.)* You will not whisper in class. You will not pass notes. You will not chew gum. If you are caught chewing gum at ANY time, you get...THE STRAP! *(Whack!)* You will do all assigned homework. I will not always ask to see your homework. If I do ask to see your homework, and it is not completed, you get...THE STRAP! *(Whack!)*

He then proceeded to "discuss" negative versus positive numeric values to us, his badly shaken students:

"Values change EVERYTHING! They change your APPROACH! They change OUTCOMES! For instance, when you subtract a positive from a positive, you will get a SMALLER NUMBER! When you subtract a negative from a negative, what will you get...THOMPSON!?"

Poor Thompson, picked at random, jumped like spit on a griddle. Swallowing audibly, he did his best to quaver out a halfway intelligent answer:

"...The strap?"*

❖   ❖   ❖

It has often been noted that when threat comes in the door, good thinking flies out the window. Recent brain research corroborates this bit of common-sense wisdom by showing how threat literally short-circuits the brain.

---

*Possibly I should note that this scenario took place in Canada, at a time when corporal punishment in schools was still an accepted procedure. If this story dates me, so be it.

When the brain perceives a threat, the usual electrical "pathways" of information are interrupted, triggering the release of stress hormones. Meanwhile, blood flow is away from the frontal lobe where creative thinking primarily takes place, and toward the midbrain and cerebellum, which are involved in more reflexive, defense/offense behaviors. All of this seriously impairs:

❖ Long-range planning

❖ Goal-setting

❖ Judgment

❖ Creative thinking

These are all processes that are imperative to learning. Picture Neanderthals eating the blackboard chalk and you've pretty much got it.

Where did this survival mechanism come from, you may ask? As with so many other brain functions, it did start with primitive humankind. Think about it: When confronted by a saber-tooth cat early in our evolution, we didn't need to get creative. ("Gee, I'd like to try a new approach this time—let's see, choices, choices...") In fact, we needed to get highly *un*creative ("Attack!" or "Run!"). As our odds for survival have dramatically increased over the ages, however, this fight-or-flight mechanism has become obsolete. Let's face it, if you've just missed your plane to Dallas for that vital meeting with your biggest client, or are about to be audited by the IRS, or just learned your company will be laying off 5,000 people, you need to start thinking more creatively, not less. Unfortunately, your brain is wired to do exactly the opposite—to get very stupid very fast. In short, this particular bit of prehistoric wiring, once meant to *keep us alive,* is counterproductive for the world today. Still, it's what we're left with.

What does this mean for teachers and trainers? Obviously that, *first and foremost, we need to eliminate high stress from our learning environments.*

Unfortunately for us, many of our learners feel an astonishing level of anxiety just by walking into our learning environments! We've all observed the enthusiasm of children as they first enter the school system, and, in most cases, their boredom and resistance by the time they are sixteen. The sad fact is that school does not seem to provide a happy, confidence-building experience for most people. This explains why, according to Colin Rose, a full four out of five teenaged and adult learners start almost every new learning experience with too-high levels of stress. They don't like being "back in school."[1]

And here is one big reason I think humor has worked so well for me: Recent studies suggest that, just as high stress short-circuits the brain, laughter short-circuits stress!

In the interesting field of psychoneuroimmunology (PNI), for example, researchers seem constantly to be giving groups of medical students comedy videos to watch, and then taking blood samples as the students are having fun. Now, you may be thinking that only medical students *could* have fun while having blood taken, and you'd probably be right, but let's let that pass. The point is, preliminary findings include increased levels of things like activated T-cells, NK cells, immunoglobulins, lymphocytes, and gamma interferon—all components of the immune system. Much more work needs to be done in this area, but signs are hopeful that "mirthful" laughter (that is, as opposed to nervous or hostile laughter, an important distinction) seems to replace negative stress ("distress") chemicals with positive stress ("eustress") ones.

> **"You don't get ulcers from what you eat. You get them from what's eating you."**
>
> **Vicki Baum,**
> novelist and playwright

More good news: Besides relieving physical stress, mirthful laughter also cuts psychological stress. The fact is that humor, used right, often moves failure forward into success. How does it do this, you ask?

Think about it for a minute. Humor is *always* about putting things together in new and unexpected ways—ways that don't quite work. Remember Carol Burnett's Scarlett O'Hara skit in Chapter 1? Think about *any* traditional joke: "I feel like the guy who had to ride his bicycle home after a vasectomy." "She's been married so often she has permanent rice scars on her face." "If a man speaks in the forest, and there's no woman to hear him, is he still wrong?" "If a woman speaks in the forest, and there's no man to hear her, is she still complaining?" Humor is never about things going the way they're supposed to! (As noted in Chapter 4, some comedians are now reversing the time-honored formula by looking at negative things and defining them as good. I find this quite fascinating, and even, in an undefined way, immensely heartening.) In my opinion, humor is Mother Nature's way of making creativity possible at all.

What do you think allowed Thomas Edison to try out 10,000 ideas in developing his light bulb? Picture it: There he is in his lab. He's investigated 9,998 substances. Most burned out within minutes; some didn't burn at all; none is burning for anything close to weeks or months, which is necessary for the light bulb to be truly useful. Edison tries out idea number 9,999. This one blows up in his face. He flings down his apparatus. "That's it!" he roars. "It can't be done!" He turns to stomp out of the lab, when suddenly he catches sight of himself in the mirror. His face is sooty; his hair is standing up, charred at the ends. He begins to laugh. He turns back to the worktable for attempt number 10,000. And eureka! The world now has electric light.

All right, so I don't know whether that exact scenario ever took place in Edison's lab. But I'll bet this year's salary that such moments have occurred in many other places at many times. The fact is that when we face our setbacks with humor, we are heartened to try again. We have received that greatest of gifts: perspective. The result is a new openness to possibilities.

> **"Life is too important to be taken seriously."**
> Oscar Wilde,
> poet and playwright

Having said all of the above, I must now admit that some negative stress can actually be a good thing in your learning environment! Appropriate kinds of distress have been found to actually enhance learning. Just be clear about the difference. *Inappropriate* distress in learning would include intense negative feelings like rage, hostility, threat, embarrassment, fear, and more. *Appropriate* distress includes things like frustration over a tough problem, a little worry or concern over an upcoming exam, some anxiety before a presentation—even disappointment or sadness after falling short of learning goals!

(Note: This last one is not so surprising if you think about it. How many times have such negative feelings provided an unforgettable learning experience for you? More than one person has said, "I learned more from my failures than from my successes." Failure brings up many negative emotions that can help propel us forward into success. Just for the record, however, let me make it clear that I do *not* suggest using, say, trick questions or impossible problems in an effort to create "desirable distress" in your learners! I only mean to show that you should not try to use humor/creativity/play in a misguided attempt to turn your classroom into some kind of unrealistic, always-happy La-La Land. To do so would only demean both humor and the learning process. Use humor/creativity/play only to circumvent the *inappropriate* forms of distress noted above.)

Reflection Section

Take ten minutes right now to describe the neural effects of stress to someone who hasn't read this chapter. (If you can't get hold of another human being at the moment, then write down the main points.) Feel free to flip back to read about anything that's not clear to you—remember, there's no such thing as cheating here, and there's no flunking out either; if you're conscious by the end of the book, you get an A!

And now, ladies and gentlemen, without further ado, here are some ways for using humor specifically to bust threat and high stress in your learning environment. These address three basic concepts:

1. Giving people a sense of choice

2. Keeping the general tone positive

3. Delivering assessment in nonthreatening ways

Let's have a look at them.

Stress-Buster #1: Give Your Learners a Sense of Choice

Choice—a.k.a. empowerment—is very much an **intrinsic motivator**. See Chap 2 Ever notice how quickly people will become listless when they have little control over their situation? Personally, I find it quite easy to believe psychologists who say that a sense of helplessness is a major cause of clinical depression. Here are two techniques for giving your learners choice.

Presentation Technique: Proactive "Show of Hands" Questions

Show-of-hands questions represent a time-honored way of letting learners "have some say" right from the start, allowing them to see that their input is valued. Meanwhile, they let you conduct a quick, informal needs assessment. The trick in this technique is to *frame your questions so that by the end everyone has raised a hand.* This will further reassure each learner that "I belong here," allowing them to **flock**. See Chap 6

WHAT TO DO

A humorous template for this is the old vaudeville one-two-three—a straight question, a second straight question, and then a "punchline" question.

For example, lest's say you are training in the new, company-wide computer system (always a fun topic). Although you know your learners may be frustrated with the old system, you may also know that some people are attached to it—if only because they don't like change. So you might ask:

1. "How many have been using our old system for more than three years?" [Show of hands.]

2. "How many have been using it for less than two years?" [Show of hands.]

3. "How many find that when you use it, you want to cry like a two-year-old?" [Show of hands, laughter.] "Just curious. So some are more comfortable with it than others. Let's talk about that for a few moments..."

Notice that in this case the punch line question allows people to get their frustrations into the open, but in a socially-sanctioned way. This will make it safe for them to voice other frustrations in the discussion that follows—a very good thing, since unspoken negativity, like a mushroom, tends to thrive in the dark. For this reason, *I always use these questions when I am aware that my learners feel negatively toward some part of their situation.* To take an obscure example that almost never happens (!), let's say your company has been acquired, and dictums are coming down from the new decision-makers at an alarming rate:

1. "How many received the outline of our new corporate vision?" [Show of hands.]

2. "How many *read* the outline of our new corporate vision?" [Show of hands.]

3. "How many *understood* the outline of our new corporate vision?" [Few or no hands go up; lots of venting laughter.]

Once again, you have made it safe for people to express their very real concerns. Now they will be more willing to listen as you address the issues: "Good! Today we're going to clear up the 'fuzzy' stuff. . . ."

Presentation Technique: Break Managers

In Chapter 9, you will see how taking regular **breaks** from learning can greatly enhance brain function. Still, you know how it goes: Sometimes we trainers get on a "roll" and forget how much time has gone by. Suddenly we notice our learners are slumping in their seats, vacant-eyed and oblivious to what we've been saying for the last fifteen minutes. So Break Managers can help you tremendously by exercising the power you bestow upon them. Think of this technique as a simple system of checks and balances.

WHAT TO DO

1. At the beginning of a training session, give one or two attendees the responsibility throughout the day of gauging when the class needs a two- or three-minute stretch break. Whenever they believe this to be the case, they must raise a hand and call, "Break!" Briefly explain to them the importance of such breaks, and how they will be doing everyone a favor by calling for them when needed.

2. Even if you've scheduled a stretch break in five minutes' time, stop immediately when the Break Manager signals. Signpost where the class is—"Okay, we'll come back to 'Interview Techniques' in two minutes"—and lead the stretch now. This will allow your students to relax, loosen up, oxygenate and, best of all, increase **attention**. Since it's optimal to change **states** gradually, these minibreaks should always start with the attendees first taking a deep breath, then sitting erect. Having moved out of their initial state ("torpor") into an intermediary state ("Oh yeah, right, I have a body"), they are now ready to move into an ideal one ("Body and brain full speed ahead").

See
Chaps 9,2

Many other techniques in this book will give your learners a sense of choice in their learning. But let's pause here for a moment. I am well aware that some teachers and trainers are far from comfortable with the idea of giving up too much control in the learning environment. This is especially true of those with recalcitrant learners. So I will now tell you a little story. Please get a drink of water, go to the bathroom, and then tuck in. . . .

HELPING LEARNERS TO MAKE POSITIVE CHOICES ABOUT THEIR LEARNING

As you may know from the introduction, I began my training career as a comedian who was hired to teach DMV-sanctioned Traffic Violator School classes (otherwise known as being "a lamb led to the slaughter"). Don't cry for me, Argentina—I learned a tremendous amount from that experience. For example, within weeks I discovered an absolutely fascinating fact of which most people are completely unaware: Only good drivers end up in traffic violator school.

Yes, it's true—ask most of them, and they'll tell you. *They're* not the ones who should be populating those high school, college, and hotel meeting rooms. It's those idiots they have to *contend* with on the road every day who should be there. They're the *real* problem. If it weren't for *them*, no one would ever be tempted to even bend a law. The whole system is ridiculously, maddeningly, insanely unjust.

Heaven knows I've often wondered how traffic officers could mess up so consistently in this area—truly, life is a mystery. But that's not the point. The point is that I started out my teaching career with the some of most resistant, defiant, *ANGRY* learners you could find anywhere.

Now, like most of my comedian/instructor colleagues, I made extensive use of theatre improvisation games as teaching tools (just as I do today, in fact). But—again like most of my colleagues—I instinctively knew that people in a rotten mood are hardly likely to take part in any kind of fun. So very quickly I made a habit of starting all of my programs with two "Anger Aikido Moves." Aikido is the martial art of going along with the opponent's momentum, and then redirecting it to advantage. My moves were similar, allowing hostility at the outset, and transforming it into a productive energy that would last throughout the day. Here are the two moves I used:

> ### ANGER AIKIDO MOVE #1: Let Them Vent
> Let learners tell you what's bugging them! Wherever possible, do this humorously (as with the "Show of Hands" questions, above), but if any individual is deeply angry, put humor aside in favor of simple, respectful listening.

This move was quite effective: People have a deep need to feel heard, and a few minutes spent satisfying that need virtually always represented a big return on investment in terms of learner participation, cooperation, and respect.

> ### ANGER AIKIDO MOVE #2: Don't Force Participation
> At the beginning of the program, assure ALL attendees that they will not have to participate in any activity that makes them feel uncomfortable!

This move was even more effective: In one fell swoop, it seemed to assuage virtually every anxiety my learners had about being "coerced" (let's remember that most of them already felt coerced into being there in the first place), while, ironically enough, making it far more likely that they actually would participate in the activities!

Still, life being the crapshoot that it is, it did not work every time. Most groups included at least one "hard case"—someone who proposed to take me at my word when I said he didn't have to participate, and who'd sit for an entire day with his arms folded firmly across his chest. Now first of all, just looking at this person was a bit of a downer for everyone else. Second, I personally wanted this person to have as good a time in my class as I knew everyone else was going to have. Third, I believed he would learn more if he enjoyed and interacted with the material. So first I sought to determine if he was shy, or just in a bad mood. If it was the former, I *let him be* (see Tip below). If it was the latter, I tried a little gag to inspire him to choose active participation.

Presentation Technique: The Wounded Trainer

WHAT TO DO

1. Let the resistant learner sit through the first activity or two. Then, at the beginning of the next learning exercise, sweetly ask *in front of everyone:* "Would you like to take part in this one?"

2. A little embarrassed, but determined to exercise the right of choice you've promised at the outset, he will usually blurt, "No, not really." (This will get an uncomfortable—albeit wickedly delighted—titter from the class.)

3. Say, "And that's *perfectly* okay."

4. Smile at him, pull a tissue from your pocket, dab at your eyes, and turn resignedly away.

Because of the *moderate stress* you've created by putting the unwilling learner "on the spot," this sight gag will get a huge laugh from everyone—including the unwilling learner! But the laugh (and your good-natured "You win, I lose" self-deprecation) will very often get the unwilling learner into a more tractable attitude. Even if he stays out of this particular learning game, in the next one he will probably roll his eyes—"Oh, what the heck"—and join in.

A TIP

This gag will only work if:

1. It suits your personal style.

2. The learner in question has an *extroverted* personality. One way to know this is if he is making something of a "show" of his resistance; if so, he is almost certainly extroverted. If he is simply being quiet, seemingly wishing to recede into the wallpaper, he is

probably more introverted, and will hate to be made the center of group attention. In this case, you should not—I repeat, *not*—use this technique. Leave him alone. It's okay. If you've created an environment of Cutting Slack (Chapter 4), he will find his own way of taking part.

3. You take any hint of manipulation out of the act. For example, during the laugh following my own demonstration of "grief," I quickly turn to my recalcitrant learner and exclaim, Joan Rivers-like, "*Just joking!!*" (You can get away with a lot of silliness with those two magical, comedy club words. Try it and see....)

Stress-Buster #2: Keep It Positive

Now that you've set the stage for a low-stress learning environment, there is a deceptively simple strategy for keeping stress low. In Chapter 4, you read about the effects of **positivity** on the brain. Of course, humor (as long as it's not the sarcastic variety) inspires positivity *par excellence*. But there are ways of keeping things positive during the more low-key moments in your presentation when you might not particularly want to inspire laughter. My favorite among these is the use of affirmations.

I have a hilarious associate named David Roche, a facially-disfigured writer, performer, and speaker who has appeared on CNN and many other media. He describes trying daily affirmations some years ago. Standing in front of his mirror he would say things like "I love myself just as I am," and "I am beautiful to me." Finally he gave it up, concluding that "affirmations are just like denial, but more work."

All witticisms aside, brain research tells us that affirmations are in fact effective brain-enhancers. Imagine, for instance, that you're holding a fresh lemon in your hand. See the dimpled, waxy skin. Squeeze the lemon. Weigh it in your hand. Smell its wonderful citrus scent. Now take a knife and cut it open. Bring one half to your mouth; bite deeply into it. Let the juice wash over your tongue....

How are you doing? Mouth watering a bit? If so, you have just proven an important point about affirmations, visualizations, and other kinds of suggestion: *The subconscious mind does not distinguish between reality and what it imagines.*

This is an important principle—and one which, ironically, we often use against ourselves. Too often we think things like, "I'm no good at this task" or "Maybe I'll fail this test." Such negative self-talk has been shown repeatedly to have a powerful, debilitating effect on both our physical state and our ability to think well. Conversely, positive imagery does the opposite. So don't avoid this seemingly kittenish technique: Use affirmations in your classroom!

Affirmations can include both oral and written statements. Let's see how both are used.

Learner Activity: Oral Affirmations

WHAT TO DO

To enhance *cooperative spirit,* you might have your teams turn to each other periodically and say any of the following:

❖ "Good to have you here."

❖ "We are one red-hot team!"

❖ "Number One and getting higher!"

❖ "Anything is possible with our genius."

❖ "I knew we were brilliant, but WOW!"

For *learning enthusiasm:*

❖ "This is what I call amazing."

❖ "I am so impressed."

❖ "Hey, this stuff is fun!"

To reinforce *key points of curriculum:*

❖ (For customer service reps:) "I'm gonna give customers more *options.*"

❖ (For managers:) "From now on I'll tell my staff the *why.*"

❖ (For desktop publishers:) "Good *graphic devices* really enhance readability."

Besides creating a positive reality for learners, oral affirmations act as rituals, helping to create **rapport**. From my experience, most learners enjoy using them. Written affirmations have the added value of presenting curriculum points peripherally or **nonconsciously** and as such are powerful mnemonics. I advise using them whenever you can.

See Chap 6

See Chap 2

Presentation Technique: Written Affirmations

Write affirmative statements on posters, and hang these on the walls all around the room. The statements should be short, positive, and emotionally phrased. Examples:

❖ "Student Exchanges between departments *work.*"

❖ "My *Difficult* Person might just be a *Different* Person."

❖ "I can verbally *ask,* and vocally *tell.*"

❖ "*Actively listen,* and the world will beat a path to your door."

As well as being received nonconsciously, affirmation posters accomplish three further brain-based objectives: They create a **state** of curiosity about the concepts they are about to learn ("What does '*actively listen*' mean?"), reinforce concepts as they learn them ("Right: *acknowledge* and *clarify.* Got it."), and create positive **emotions**.

See Chap 2

See Chap 3

Stress-Buster #3: Keep Assessment Nonthreatening

Quick story: Once, while standing in a supermarket checkout line, my eye was caught by one of those tiny, impulse-item books they so cunningly place in front of the register. Its title: *How to Train Your Cat.* Intrigued, I picked the book up and opened to page one. It contained a single line, which read, "Rule 1: When issuing your cat a command, try to make it something the animal is already planning to do." The rest of the page—and the book—was blank.

I howled with glee (not something you want to do too often in a super-market, it turns out), but later, I thought seriously about the biological realities behind the joke. The reason that cats are less trainable than dogs is not so much because they are less intelligent, as because *dogs are a flock-ing species, while cats are not.* Dogs and their ilk (wolves, jackals, dingoes, and so on) tend to travel in packs. For this reason, dogs' brains are wired to recognize hierarchy, to take their lead from an "Alpha" dog. Training a dog is essentially an exercise in establishing yourself as this "Alpha" so that the dog wants to please you. Most species of cats, on the other hand (lions being one high-profile exception), are solitary. As such, they have no "Alpha" wiring. They do not connect pleasing with receiving. In their minds, any benefits they receive in life are just the luck of the draw.

We human beings are a flocking species. This means that *as group leader, on some level you are seen as the "Alpha."* In my experience this is always true, whether my learners be phone staff, district attorneys, uni-versity professors, or vice presidents of multinationals. Claiming Alpha status can be a bit daunting, especially at first, but I have found this is got-ten over fairly easily by remembering that some 80 percent of profession-als suffer from "Impostor Syndrome," the belief that they are neither knowledgeable nor experienced enough to act as authorities. Anytime I have felt that kind of insecurity creeping in, I've looked closely at the qual-ity of my work. If it was up to standard, then I would conclude, "This is nothing but Impostor Syndrome!" For some reason this would always comfort me, and I could forge ahead.

Okay, so knowing that your role is essentially that of the Alpha, you must recognize that your learners—even if they are more highly educated than you and make twice your salary—are likely to give added weight to your opinion of them, simply because you are the teacher. As Keirsey and

Bates say: "Whatever our temperaments, we are all social creatures, and so want to please the boss."[2] This means that you must deliver your assessments with care; if you are overly somber or critical, your learners won't be able to "hear" you.

The most effective (and nonthreatening) assessment comes in the form of *corrective feedback during the process,* rather than judgment after the fact. In other words, the back-and-forth that occurs between you and your learners is probably the best way for both to see how well they are grasping the material.

Here are two ways to encourage more back-and-forth, allowing you to assess their work, and also to give them corrective feedback in ways they can "hear." The two ways are: 1) active listening and 2) respond, respond, respond!

ACTIVE LISTENING

Active listening allows you not only to listen better, but also to better *convey to your learners that you are listening* (which in itself provides them with a subtle, positive "assessment," if you think about it). It involves showing them that you hear and understand them, rather than just letting them assume so. After all, you could be the best listener in the world, but if your style of listening involves merely attentive silence, the person speaking to you may not know for sure whether you're really receiving their communication, or just staring at them while secretly thinking, "Did I turn the stove off this morning?"

> **"The basic thing which contributes to charm is the ability to forget oneself and be engrossed in other people."**
> Eleanor Roosevelt,
> American First Lady

Active listening involves two behaviors:

1. Acknowledging (communicating that you hear)

2. Clarifying (communicating that you understand)

Acknowledging means you give signals that say, "I got that." You acknowledge a speaker's *main points,* either by nodding or saying things like, "M-hm," "I see," "Aha," "Yes," "Okay," and so on. Each time you do this with a main point, your speaker feels heard.

Clarifying means you ask the *who-how-what-where-when* questions. "What do you mean when you say. . . ?" "How did you learn to do that?" "What happened when. . . ?" and so on. As you make the effort to clarify, your speaker feels better understood.

Trainer Practice: Active Listening

WHAT TO DO

1. Together with a colleague, decide who has the longer fingers. That will be Person A; the other will be Person B.

2. Person A tells Person B about some special skill, interest, or talent they have, and describes how they developed their expertise in this particular area. Person B listens, interjecting acknowledgements of the salient points.

3. At the end of Person A's story, Person B asks two or three clarifying questions on points about which they are still curious. *Examples:* "How old were you when you discovered this talent for drawing?" "Where do you go in the city to do rock-climbing?", etc.

4. Switch off, letting Person B tell about their interest, while Person A listens actively.

DEBRIEF

❖ When you used the twin tactics of acknowledging and clarifying, did you find that you listened better—heard and understood more—than you usually do? If so, does this fact alone provide you with a good reason to actively listen in all your interactions?

❖ When you told your story, what did it feel like to have someone listen in so focused a manner? How often do people in your daily life listen to you this way?

❖ Thinking about it, you knew your partner was listening as part of an exercise—hey, maybe they were secretly bored stiff. But do you find that it *still* felt great to be listened to? *Key Point:* Other people will feel the same way when you actively listen to them!

RESPOND, RESPOND, RESPOND!

This one is subtle. It is based on the fact that the way you respond to your learners' input will be taken by them as tacit evaluations. Specifically, do you seem to respond to *them*, or just to their question or comment? Do you pause for a second, thank them for contributing, make solid eye contact, speak with energy? All these things will tell your learners that they have your friendly attention and interest—and it is impossible to feel threatened when that's the case.

And herein lies possibly the best reason for building your humor skills. Once again, humor is not about focusing in but focusing out. As you work at this wonderful art, even when you don't try to be funny you will find that people smile and laugh more in your presence. They feel engaged with you; you seem so obviously to like them, to value their presence. They relax, they feel positive and hopeful—and surprise, surprise, their performance improves.

So share your spotlight generously! Make it your first order of business that *all learner input receives your sincere appreciation.* Give resounding "Thank you!"s, "Exactly!"s, "Perfect!"s (or at least "Not bad!"s), for their contributions. Always offer an appreciative laugh at their humor (assuming it's appropriate; see Chapter 10). And if they say something funny that the others didn't hear, *definitely* repeat the comment to the group at large, all the while pointing at the speaker to give that person the credit. (This one pays huge dividends, believe me.) Respond-respond-respond—and they will do the same back to you.

Making Sure Exams Measure Mastery, Not Fear

No discussion of threat would be complete without discussing exams. Every teaching professional knows how exams can have an astonishing capacity to liposuction the knowledge right out of students. Again, although a moderate amount of stress ("I really *want* to do well") can actually improve learner performance, excessive stress ("I *have* to do well—but I don't think I will") has the opposite effect.

Virtually all of the techniques in this book will serve to lighten the exam-writing atmosphere by teaching learners to Cut Themselves Some Slack, or by creating that enviable **state** of "Knowing They Know." Still, exam scores often feel (and often are) crucial to our learners, since they can spell the difference between getting or losing the passing grade, the scholarship, the job, the certification, or the promotion. Use state-specific reviews and self-management tools to alleviate excess stress, and to keep their brains from "short-circuiting" in the exam environment.

See
Chap 2

Presentation Technique: State-Specific Review #1— "Where Were You When...?"

See
Chap 2

Remember the **Episodic pathway**? It allows us to remember information by returning to the *physical location* in which we learned it. This happens because many of the associations we formed around the material were **nonconscious** ones of place and experience. You can use this pathway to great advantage.

See
Chap 2

WHAT TO DO

Whenever possible, have your learners take their exams in the same room, *and even the same seats,* in which they learned the material. If they have moved since that part of the program, a good way to help them find their original seats is to ask, "Where were you sitting when we learned about (some colorful or humorous bit of curriculum)?" They will almost certainly find their seats immediately.

(By the way, besides jogging their memories, this will also give them greater confidence in their Episodic pathways—helping them to "know that they know.")

Presentation Technique: State-Specific Review #2— Suffer Sessions

We also use the Episodic pathway in re-experiencing the *emotional circumstances* surrounding our learning. This means that, when necessary, you should build the experiential circumstance of exam-taking into your learning by making some of your reviews simulate the actual exam experience—in essence, giving your learners "stress rehearsal."

WHAT TO DO

1. Impose silence.

2. Hand out exams similar to those they will have to complete at the end of the course.

3. Give strict time limits for completion; do not allow talking; generally create a tense atmosphere.

4. After the exam, go over the answers, take questions, invite discussion. Make sure everyone feels confident they know the material.

5. Debrief the stressful experience with your learners.

DEBRIEF

❖ How did it feel to take an exam?

❖ If it made you nervous, do you think that had an impact on your performance?

❖ How many feel you know the material we just reviewed? *Key Point:* How many realize you knew it better than you thought you did while you were taking the exam?

❖ What can you do to cut stress during real exams?

A TIP

Introduce the above rehearsals humorously as "Suffer Sessions"—and always explain to your learners why they're engaging in them: so that they are not thrown by your suddenly becoming "Captain Bly." In fact if it suits your style, why not appear at these sessions wearing a black robe and mortarboard, and perhaps even carrying a small riding crop? This in no way eliminates the stress of the experience, although it does reduce it to manageable levels, which they can then recreate when taking the real exam.

ANOTHER TIP

If you do show up with a robe and whip, get rid of both after the first couple of minutes. After that it will start to get creepy, both for them and you.

Presentation Technique: Self-Management Tools

WHAT TO DO

A FEW DAYS BEFORE THE EXAM Give your learners a list of traditional test-taking strategies (go with your first answer, leave difficult questions behind and come back to them later, etc.). Better yet, let them practice these strategies in the above-mentioned "rehearsal" exam.

THE DAY OF THE EXAM

1. Lead your learners in relaxation breathing:
   * Place a hand on the abdomen just under the navel.
   * Intentionally breath down "into" the hand, consciously making the lower abdomen inflate before the chest.
   * Hold the breath for two to four seconds. Notice the moment of stillness, and how easy it is for the mind to focus on this single action.
   * Exhale, and again hold for two to four seconds. Again, notice the stillness.
   * Repeat five or six times

2. Lead your learners in affirmations and other positive self-talk:
   * "I have learned a lot, and will do well in this exam."
   * "I've done good work in this class, and am confident I know the material."

Consider adding a couple of funnier ones, like:

❖ *"Gee,* I'm good!"

❖ "If only everyone were as smart as me!"

3. Lead your learners in a visualization:

❖ "I'm proud of the effort I've put into this course. I have loads of information at my fingertips—even more than I realize! As I take the test, the answers come easily. Each question triggers my memory to work almost effortlessly. As I continue through the test, I am amazed at how easy it is. I enjoy proving how much I know."

Reflection Section

Are there any issues that may be triggering high stress in your learners? What would these be? If you don't know, can you ask around to find out? Which of the above techniques do you think would help ease your learners' concerns? Have you got any others of your own? Write them down now.

....

....

....

....

....

....

....

....

....

Some Next Steps

1. Do a little sleuthing to find out whether your learners feel threatened about any aspect of their training. If so, plan strategies to lower their stress.

2. Buy a pocket package of tissue to use as "The Wounded Trainer."

3. Think about some funny reasons trainees might want to attend your programs. Is there anything you've heard them say in the hall or the coffee room? Is there anything you've learned through the "grapevine"? Get ready to use it to advantage with your proactive "Show of Hands" questions!

4. Practice the two steps of Active Listening in every conversation for the next week. Make it a habit as quickly as possible!

5. For one week, practice responding to other people's comments with more energy: "Aha!," "Yes!," "I see," "Very nice," etc.

6. (Only if this suits your personal style:) Buy a black robe, mortarboard, and riding crop to wear during "Suffer Sessions."

You have just learned some guaranteed methods for reducing stress among your listeners. One last time: Remember that it is only high stress we want to avoid in learning. Do *not* use humor to try to jolly your learners into some sort of blissful Stepford Wives-like contentment. Let them experience moderate levels of stress. Let them make mistakes, let them try and fail, let them worry a little over things like presentations, quizzes, and exams, and beating the other learning teams. This is healthy and brain-compatible—just as long as failing does not lead to feeling like a failure.

And now on to Chapter 6, where we'll discuss using humor to fulfill a particularly vital—and oft-ignored—learning imperative. . .

drawing people together to enlist "the social brain"

CHAPTER 6

IN THE PRECEDING chapter, you saw how important it is to eliminate threat from your learning environment. It seems the brain needs to feel we are safe in order to free up the neural circuitry nec-

❝The classroom is as much a social situation as an academic one.❞

Daniel Goleman, emotional intelligence guru

are safe in order to free up the neural circuitry necessary for optimal learning. Probably the foremost safety need we "flocking" humans have is to feel *included in the group.* Before we can feel that way, however, we first need to feel that it's a safe group to be included in! Your learners will want to be included in your group if you address the three top items on their "Safety Agenda":

1. The credibility of the leader

2. The approachability of the leader

3. Rapport with peers

Let's take these one at a time.

Safety Item #1: Your Credibility

Professional communicators of all kinds are deeply concerned about the issue of "credibility"—indeed, put two of them together in a room for five minutes and the word will almost certainly come up. And with good reason: It is all-important that our listeners can respect our knowledge and authority as well as our teaching ability. Still, many highly competent communicators seem to feel the need to over-assert their expert status, usually through some variation of excessively formal behavior. Some overdress for the occasion, some maintain a fierce grip on their laser pointer at all times and never come down from the podium, *many* take great pains to reveal their numerous accreditations and accomplishments. And so it goes. . . .

Interestingly enough, it is actually an *informality,* what I call a "Wide Comfort Zone," that defines the confident, truly credible person. Think of some of the most beloved—and respected—public figures of the last century: Will Rogers, Walter Cronkite, Betty Ford, Ronald Reagan, Princess Diana, Oprah Winfrey. Now imagine yourself accidentally placing one of your presentation overheads face-down on the projector screen, and instead of gulping, "Oops, sorry!" you intone: "Hmmmmmm. Defective." In laughing at your mistake rather than being embarrassed by it, you immediately come across as self-assured, yet human and approachable. You seem secure in both yourself and your ability to face the unexpected— Ta-Da!—and people feel a higher level of security and trust around you.

Two good ways to demonstrate your credibility with lightness and wit are through:

1. Straight talk (i.e., colloquial language)

2. Self-deprecating humor

STRAIGHT TALK

By far, one of the most common excessive formalities many communicators adopt is a somewhat officious verbal style. I frankly call this "playing Grown-up." Now, most of us would recoil at the suggestion that we are playing at anything, and I certainly don't mean to insult. But just in case you're curious about your own tendencies in this direction, here's a quick self-test: Have you ever said "utilize" instead of "use"? "Administer" instead of "give"? "Necessity" instead of "need"? If so, then you have played Grown-up at least once. Welcome to the club! I am reminded here of a brilliant lawyer I know of personally, who read a draft written by an associate in his firm and determined that it was too wordy. His penciled note: "Strive to maximize verbal efficiency"! I don't suggest that this man was intentionally seeking to astonish the associate with his erudite vocabulary, only that his professional training had perhaps instilled a tendency toward excessively ceremonial locution. . .um, I mean, fancy talk.

Why not do a quick exercise right now to build your own verbal IQ (Informality Quotient)? It will take two minutes, and it certainly won't hurt you. . . .

Trainer Practice: Keep It Simple

Rewrite the following statements to make them shorter. Then check your answers with the suggested answers given at the end of the exercise (Note: They don't have to match perfectly.)

1. A case study can be likened to a written demonstration.

   ....

2. To be an effective teaching professional, it is imperative that one regularly bestows appropriate praise and positive feedback on those being taught.

   ....

3. Those speakers who are perceived as "personable" usually seem to possess a flair for spontaneity.

   ....

4. In any discussion of leadership, it is of primary importance to acknowledge the significance of listening.

   ....

(*Answers:* 1. A case study is like a written demonstration. 2. Effective teachers regularly give appropriate praise and positive feedback. OR: If you want to be effective, give a few strokes! 3. Truly personable speakers are spontaneous. OR: If you want audiences to pay attention, liven up. 4. Good leaders listen.)

Again, your answers do not have to match mine; indeed, mine may not be the best for a given context. The idea here is to realize that you can usually make your case with fewer and shorter words than you thought. Which of the above statements are easier to remember, the longer ones, or the rewritten, shorter ones? Which would feel less intimidating to a learner without an advanced college degree? Come to that, which would sound less pompous to discriminating learners with advanced college degrees? Point made, I hope.

SELF-DEPRECATING HUMOR

Another way in which communicators may seek to convey "authority" is by constantly referring to their accreditations and achievements. I do not suggest here that your listeners should *not* know about your accomplishments, but only that you should not continually broadcast them: It's pompous and annoying, and if anything, makes you look less sure of yourself. You know what you've accomplished; if your learners don't strike you as being properly impressed, you will hardly inspire their admiration with chest beating. To the contrary, you will do better by taking the example of the beloved leaders noted above, and develop a Wide Comfort Zone—a talent for the "Ta-Da."

> **"Wear your learning like a pocket watch, and keep it hidden. Do not pull it out to count the hours, but give the time when you are asked."**
> Lord Chesterfield,
> eighteenth-century British guy

One of the best "Ta-Da"s you can use is self-deprecating humor. This technique is successful largely because it is proactive: You do not wait for a mistake to prove your fallibility, but in fact announce beforehand that you are fallible! By presenting yourself at the outset as just another human being, you can immediately reduce distance between yourself and your listeners—putting everyone, so to speak, on the same side. As one excellent example, Mario Cuomo once started off an address to the New York Press Club: "As I left to come here tonight, my wife said, 'I know it's a difficult subject and a tough group, but don't be intimidated. And don't try to be charming, witty, or intellectual. Just be yourself.'"

Here is a game through which you can practice self-deprecating humor. Essentially, it is a reverse of the game *"Fortunately"* from Chapter 4. Like that game, it involves what comedians call "turn-about" humor, finding reasons that good things are bad and bad things are good. Unlike that game, however, you are now going to focus on why good things are bad. You've undoubtedly used this kind of humor countless times, like when you've thrilled at a tax refund check, and then said, "Hey, wait a minute—this was my money to start with!" So this game should come easy to you. I call it:

Trainer Practice: What, You Thought I Was Einstein?
WHAT TO DO

1. Think of specific things about yourself that might intimidate your learners. For example, if you have an extremely high level of expertise in your topic, some of them might realistically expect a bit of condescension from you. Or if you are the one who determines whether or not they will "make the grade"—get the job, raise, or promotion—they might legitimately hesitate to ask questions, make mistakes, or volunteer for activities.

2. Now try some turn-about humor to knock these intimidators down to size. What is *bad* about your having all that knowledge and power? Remember, every silver lining has a cloud! Some ways to seek out the "cloud":

   ❖ *Find a Common Enemy:* Identify your learners' feelings (in this case, the fear that they will fail), and see if you can apply those same feelings to yourself in any way: "I just reread my job description, and saw that if you folks don't do well *I'm* officially classified as a lousy teacher. So believe me, I'm going to do everything I can to help everyone master the material. . . ."

   ❖ *Rent-a-Cloud:* Think about authority figures you yourself have known in the past: Have any of them had a chink anywhere in their armor? Put that chink in your own: "Some of you may have known Ph.D.s who have done brilliant research, but can't tie their own shoelaces. I want to put your fears about my competency to rest right now." *[Bend down and tie a shoe.]* "Okay, with that out of the way, let us move on. . . ."

❖ *Random Access:* If nothing else succeeds, this quick technique will almost always help you find those unexpected connections that create humor. Open a book, magazine, or newspaper, point to a word, and try to connect it with the idea that your knowledge and power are bad.

Example: Let's say you point to the word "twins." Start listing other words or phrases that come to mind, like identical, Siamese, Gemini, and so on. If none of them gives you an idea about why power is bad, continue playing with them: Gemini, horoscope, "What's your sign?", singles bar, dating. . . . How about, "I am senior manager of waste management here at _____. I also teach graduate classes in Industrial Chemistry at Drexel. And as you may well imagine, if I weren't already married these two things would get me a *lot* of dates."

DEBRIEF

❖ That last turn-about comment is not necessarily the best one you could come up with. It is, however, the first halfway funny one *I* came up with in playing this game right now. You might also be interested to know that the first word I tried was "restaurant." After getting nothing from fast food, French, Italian, cook, waiter, and so on, I discarded it and tried "twins." The whole exercise took about fifteen minutes.

❖ Note that in none of the above examples have you said, "I am not competent," but only, "I do not require that you to fall down and worship me." As well you shouldn't!

TIP

While self-effacing humor can neutralize unfriendly feelings as if by magic, there is one caveat: *It only works if you are a person of perceived authority.* In our society, for example, self-deprecating humor has been known to backfire on women—even women in acknowledged positions of authority! Interestingly enough, this often apparently has less to do with societal bias than with the fact that these women nonverbally "signal" a deficit of confidence.[1]

Assuming they exhibit the self-assurance attendant on their position, however, women—and anyone else—can use self-deprecating humor to great advantage. Any speaker wishing to try the disarming technique of self deprecation should first examine their overall style. If it is fairly forceful— including a well-carrying voice, a tendency to end sentences on a downward inflection, unhurried delivery, and strong body language (not too much hand waving or head wagging)—they will have no problem, and this technique is definitely one they should have in their arsenal.

There is an old fable about a giant who had married a human-sized woman. Although small, his wife possessed a fiery temper, and, when enraged, would grab the nearest broom or pot and beat him unmercifully about the ankles and feet. The giant could easily have subdued her with a sweep of his massive hand. But she was the love of his life. So instead, he placidly acknowledged her attacks with the same fond response: "Go ahead—it doesn't hurt me, and it makes you feel better."

When you refuse to play Grown-up, and even playfully knock yourself down to size for the comfort of your learners, you make yourself into that giant. After all, you are the one in charge. Members of any group—no matter at what level—need to feel they can rely on their leader, and this is far easier to do with a leader who appears relaxed and confident. In your position, you do not have the luxury of being humorless. You must be willing to laugh at yourself. So go ahead: It won't hurt you, and it will make them feel better.

We've seen some light-touch ways of demonstrating your credibility. Now let's look at how humor can make your listeners feel safe with you.

Safety Item #2: Your Approachability

I know I am hardly the first trainer who has faced unwilling and even hostile learners. (In fact, if you read the introduction to this book, you know just how hostile some of my driving-school attendees were!) How do many of us typically respond in such challenging situations? Again, by stiffening up, protecting our curriculum from covert, or even overt, attacks. Yet here is where the phenomenal power of humor really comes through—in anticipating and defusing resistance to your topic.

In Malcolm Kushner's book *The Light Touch: How to Use Humor for Business Success* (tragically, now out of print, although it can be had on audio tape[2]), he describes a group of tax collectors who needed to respond to a frequently asked question at public-information seminars: "Why do tax forms have to be so #@$%&!!#! complicated?" The tax collectors could have responded honestly that, for better or worse, the design of our tax forms is dictated by the legislature. But this would hardly have mitigated bad feeling! So instead they worked up this humorous reply: "Tax forms are complicated because they're designed by the same people who write instructions for assembling children's toys." After bringing their audience onto their side with humor, they were then able to give the real answer, which their attendees accepted with relative equanimity.

> **"A smile is the shortest distance between two people.**
> Victor Borge,
> concert pianist and humorist

Significantly, before hitting on their winning response, the tax collectors went through a number of unusable gags: "Tax forms are really a secret government IQ test"; "They're actually quite simple if you don't earn any income"; "Don't worry, we've got a new one for people like you— you just connect the dots!" Yet, funny as they were, what was the problem with all of these comebacks? *They seemed to make fun of the questioners.* In their winning answer, the tax collectors did what you learned in "What, You Thought I Was Einstein?"—they got themselves onto the same side as their listeners by creating a Common Enemy. In their case, it was toy assembly manuals. Very nice work.

Why not try this tactic out yourself—or maybe with your training team? Here's a game I call:

Trainer Practice: Light Answers to Heavy Questions

HOW TO PLAY

1. With your training team, think of an irritable question you've all heard from learners many times, and know you'll hear again.

2. Start thinking up off-the-wall answers to these predictable questions. Remember: At this stage you don't need to worry about your ideas being brilliant—Ta-Da! Even hostile answers, although inappropriate for actual use, are okay for now. As hostile as your rejects are, do you think your team will get a laugh out of them? Definitely! You will vent your own frustrations in private, at the same time bonding with each other by poking fun at *your* Common Enemy. Maybe this is your organization's competitors or partners, maybe a state legislative or standards agency, maybe the learners themselves, maybe other departments in your organization, or even the people at the top (remember that open expression of genuine frustration is *very* good for an organization, since negativity, like a mushroom, thrives in the dark).

3. After privately venting your own hostility together, settle your thinking caps and start looking over your snappy comebacks. See if any of them can be reworded to poke fun at a) yourselves, or b) the "enemy" you share with your learners. If they can, you've got your funny answer.

IMPORTANT TIP

Be sure always to give your learners the real answer immediately after the funny one. Otherwise, you will look as if you're dismissing the question, and your humor will get a reputation as being manipulative.

You have just gone a long way in building rapport between your learners and you. Now for two techniques you can count on to build instant rapport between your learners and their curriculum:

Presentation Technique: Start Your Program with a Joke

I know, I know. All the way back in Chapter 1, I said joke telling is not necessary for bringing humor into your presentations. And I meant it. Still, this is indisputably a tried-and-true speaking presentation technique, and as such does not bear omission. Although jokes do constitute only a small part of what we daily experience as humor, they can serve beautifully in getting "buy-in." They can also enhance memory by engaging **emotion**, and, in the best cases, providing a great **metaphor** for your topic.

See
Chap 8
&
Chap 9

A TIP

Jokes, more than some other kinds of humor, must relate directly to the topic at hand. If they don't, I guarantee your attendees will remember the jokes over the curriculum. If, for example, your topic is "Customer Service" and you tell, say, a political joke, your attendees' attention will turn away from customer service and toward politics, since you've just made that the more **intrinsically motivating** topic. So if you do choose to use jokes, choose discriminatingly! Some good sources for business-oriented humor are listed in the bibliography of this book. Meanwhile, Chapter 11 gives you practice in comic delivery.

See
Chap 2

Okay, so let's say that you (like most people) don't want to tell jokes—never have, never will. Good news! You can let someone else do it for you! How about this easy alternative:

Presentation Technique: Use Relevant Cartoons on Overheads and Handouts

Essentially, cartoons are just pictorial jokes. Cool: This means that besides engaging emotion and creating metaphors, they also make use of that all-powerful **visual memory**. *Key point:* Use them, darn it!

See
Chap 7

WHAT TO DO

1. Clip out any and all cartoons you come across that relate to

your topic(s). Note that like jokes, cartoons must relate *directly and consciously* to the topic you are addressing.

2. Keep a file, and draw from it frequently.

3. Build a reputation as a teacher who likes cartoons! Learners will soon start to give far more attention to your overheads and handouts. They will start to bring you cartoons. They will be flattered when you use them.

A TIP

Unlike jokes, published cartoons are copyrighted material. As such, they may only be legally used in "face-to-face" teaching—in other words, within your physical classroom. Using them in Web-based training, for example, could get you or your organization into hot water. So can photocopying and handing them out. Still, you can always request permission from the publisher to use cartoons. Find their phone number on the masthead of the publication in which you found the cartoon, and ask for the Permissions Department. You might be surprised when they say "Yes"! If you are unsure about the legality of your own use of cartoons (or any other reprinted material), copy shops often keep booklets on the premises explaining your rights and restrictions.

Safety Item #3: Rapport Among Your Learners

We've looked at some ways to initiate rapport *with* your learners. Two ways to build rapport *among* your learners are through flocking and peer feedback. Let's see how we can satisfy these two primal human needs.

FLOCKING

As noted in Chapter 5, we are perhaps first and foremost a gregarious species. This means that, before almost anything else, we need to feel included in our group. In case you didn't know, advertising is founded on this principle. Just turn off the sound during TV commercials, and you'll quickly see the subliminal messages: Want to be more popular? More beloved by your family and friends? Sexier? Eat _____ Peanut Butter!

I, of course, exhort you to use your knowledge of flocking only for good, Grasshopper. The fact that the brain is a social organ means that *your learners will think and work better when they feel included in the learning community.* Following are three fun, effective techniques for making people feel included.

Presentation Technique: Quirky Show-of-Hands Questions

We all use show-of-hands questions at the beginning of a presentation to create a sense of commonality and involvement: "How many have lots of experience in accounting? How many have limited experience? And how many wish it would go away?" I personally continue throughout my programs with more playful, but still to-the-point, questions:

"Premise: Humans have more similarities than differences. For instance, how many get a surge of pride when you change lanes on the freeway—and don't hit any of the divider bumps? See—we're all alike!"

Or: "I need team leaders. How many at one time in your life believed Mt. Rushmore was a natural phenomenon? For being good Americans, you're our leaders!"

Each time I do this, team feeling escalates and general energy bumps up a notch.

Other examples of quirky questions might be:

❖ "How many have successfully defended 'your' clothes dryer from someone who wanted to use it at the laundromat?"

❖ "How many can't bring yourselves to use the last sheet of facial tissue in the box, because that will mean you'll have to go out and buy a new box?"

❖ "How many have ever gone to the store for milk and bread, and come back with a waffle iron, toothpicks, potato chips, bathroom stick-ons, a calendar, and guacamole—but forgot the milk and bread?"*

TIPS

❖ You can easily come up with a Quirky Things list of your own. Think about those quirky things *you* do (preferring the toilet paper installed rolling forward instead of back) or have done (sneaking eleven items through the Nine Item check-out lane, etc., etc., etc.). Then ask friends and colleagues if they do the same. If several say yes, you've got a show of hands question!

❖ A particularly enjoyable way to get a Quirky Things list is to take a tongue-in-cheek poll at parties or other social gatherings. Tell everyone honestly that you need the information for a class you are designing. They will be intrigued, and will usually feel a great desire to contribute. There will be laughs of delight as they come up with ideas. (Value-added bonus: You will be seen as someone with a wonderful gift for "breaking the ice." Trust me, people love this stuff!)

Presentation Technique: The Standard Phrase

This "weird little wonder" is subtle, yet can be used to good effect throughout your program. The Standard Phrase can 1) signpost key points, while 2) becoming a sort of signature for you. Examples of the Standard Phrase include:

1. Before or after key points:

❖ "Okay, Sensation Seekers"

❖ "It's a *good* thing" (á la Martha Stewart)

❖ "Hear me now and believe me later" (Hans and Franz from *Saturday Night Live*)

*A tip of the hat to Lily Tomlin and Jane Wagner for this one.

2. After recaps or at the end of a module:

❖ "That's a wrap" (film director)

❖ "Fall out" (drill sergeant)

❖ "Hey—let's be *careful* out there" (Sergeant from *Hill Street Blues*)

❖ "Now go and sin no more" (one of my college professors)

Key Point: Find common, recognizable phrases from film, TV, literature, or other forms of popular culture. Assuming they fit with your personal style, these phrases seem to tickle attendees, who will many times use them back to you.

Presentation Technique: Messing with Time

If there's one thing learners learn, it's to expect time limits on work. So why not make this an opportunity for flocking? Instead of telling people they have five minutes to discuss a topic with their Study Buddies, ten minutes to work on an exercise or prepare for an activity, or fifteen minutes for a break, give them unusual amounts of time. For instance, say: "You now have six minutes to discuss," or "I'll give you nine-and-a half minutes to prepare," or "Please return from break in exactly fifteen-point-three minutes." This whimsical technique will always get a smile, meanwhile giving your learners an easy "inside joke" to share. You will hear them in the halls, the restrooms, the cafeteria, and elsewhere, saying, "Better hurry—we've only got two-point-seven minutes!"

PEER FEEDBACK

Peer feedback is an excellent flocking device. Feedback is a big intrinsic motivator—the brain just likes knowing how it's doing— as long as it is regular, timely, and clear. Ideally, feedback should come at thirty-minute intervals (think how few learning environments offer that!), which means that *your learners can often get more frequent and timely feedback from each other than from you.* The following activities are particularly powerful, since they allow for both flocking and quality feedback—and in addition are tailor-made to **celebrate** learning success, as you will shortly see. For all these reasons, I emphatically suggest that you use them whenever you can.

See Chap 2

Learner Activity: Teams

Get your attendees into learning teams as early as possible in your program. The best team size is five to seven people. Two light-touch ways to create teams are:

FOR LARGER GROUPS

1. Divide the number of attendees by 5 or 7, and then have them count off. Example: If you have, say, twenty-eight attendees, you can have four teams with seven members each. Have your learners count off, "One!" "Two!" "Three!" "Four!" until everyone has a number.

2. Have learners find their number partners and form their teams.

3. Tell the Ones, "Okay, now say, 'We're number One!'" They will usually do so immediately and enthusiastically.

4. Turn to the Twos: "Now *you* guys say, 'We're number Two!'—Oh, wait a minute. That's not quite as much fun, is it?" This always gets a healthy laugh, and puts learners in the mood for the next step, finding a team name.

FOR SMALLER GROUPS

1. Point to opposite sides of the room, and say, "Creamy or chunky?" Most times, attendees will know exactly what you're talking about.

2. Have the people who prefer chunky peanut butter move to one side of the room, and the ones who prefer creamy congregate on the opposite side.

TIPS

❖ Other preferences by which people are pretty evenly divided are: "Mayonnaise or Miracle Whip," "Seinfeld or Frasier," "West Wing" or "Survivor," "Beatles or Rolling Stones," "Britney or Christina". . .the list is endless—you can easily come up with more of your own.

❖ "Ad lib" idea: If a learner says, "I hate both those choices!" just laugh and then say, "I applaud your honesty. In that case, just pick the one you hate the least."

❖ Workplace-specific choices get a particularly good response because they make everyone feel like an "insider." For instance, pick two popular menu items from the company cafeteria— "Monday foccacia or Friday chili?"—or two organizational events—"Christmas party or Family Day?"—and watch team feeling rise.

❖ If you don't get two fairly equally-sized teams, invite a couple of people from the larger one to be "Honorary Chunkies" (or whatever), and join the other team. (Another "ad lib" idea: Sometimes they will say in mock horror, "Chunky? No way!" I like to commiserate: "I know. It's a great sacrifice you're being asked to make for the good of the group. Chunkies, give them a hand for their selflessness!" The smaller team will usually applaud their new team members good-naturedly, the new members will smilingly join their new compatriots, and a little preliminary team bonding will have taken place.)

Learner Activity: Team Names

Learning teams seem to enjoy naming themselves, a deceptively simple act that creates communal feeling almost instantly. The secret is not to make a big thing of it, so that your learners don't feel you're treating them like children.

WHAT TO DO

1. Once your teams have formed, say something like, "And now take two-and-three-quarter minutes to give your team a name so I'll know what to call you." Turn away and start shuffling your notes.

2. After the allotted time has passed, use a noisemaker (Chapter 10) to get everyone's attention.

3. Have the teams share their names with the rest of the class. Write these down on a flip chart or whiteboard, with columns underneath.

Guaranteed: There will always be at least one or two teams who give themselves funny names. Your job, of course, is to lead the applause when this happens. This will lighten the atmosphere in general, and inspire the others to try their own hand at creativity as your program continues. It's also another way for you to focus *out*, letting them be "part of the act." (By the way, my all-time favorite team name to date is "Bob." If your learners are half as funny, you've got a fabulous group. Note: Be sure to tell them so!)

Here's another flocking activity that works particularly well in informal and motivational settings:

Learner Activity: Team Cheers

As well as a name, ask your teams to come up with a team cheer. Then be prepared: Most will come up with some of the oddest "cheers" you've ever heard! Appropriate times for teams to use their cheers:

❖ When they've finished a presentation

❖ When they've met any objective they listed on their Goal Assessment chart (Chapter 9)

❖ When they've won a learning competition (Chapter 7)

Actually, there is no inappropriate time for teams to cheer themselves. This act of **celebration** adds a great positive energy to the day's proceedings, helps your learners' brains hold onto what they've just learned, and makes them want to learn more.

See Chap 2

VITAL TIP

Team cheers tend not to go over well with what, in Meyers-Briggs terms, we might call "TJ" learners—executives, analysts, accountants, programmers and so on![3] These personality types, with their strong linguistic and cognitive thinking aptitudes, usually feel personally insulted if they think their learning environment has in any way been "dumbed down." If your attendees fall into this category, I'd advise you to forgo this activity. But don't worry: Just like everyone else, these folks prefer to have fun wherever possible, and will respond positively to many other humorous tactics in this book.

Reflection Section

Do you ever play "Grown-up" with your learners? What are some terms, expressions, and jargon you could replace with more everyday language? Also, can you think of any nonverbal behaviors by which you might signal a lack of credibility—even when you know exactly what you're talking about and doing? What are these behaviors? More importantly, what do you need to do differently to "come across" as the expert you are?

On a scale of 1 to 10, how would you rate yourself in creating rapport *with* your learners? How do you put your learners at ease at the beginning of a program? How do you make yourself approachable throughout?

On a scale of 1 to 10, how would you rate yourself in creating rapport *among* your learners? What opportunities do you give them to flock? Where and when? Are there any flocking techniques of your own that you've thought about trying? Does the above information encourage you to put them into practice? Does it give you any ideas for modification?

....

....

....

....

....

....

Some Next Steps

1. Start a contest with your teaching colleagues: Write out a "heavy" learner question everyone in your groups has heard, post it on the coffee room bulletin board, and invite light answers. Funniest usable answer wins two tickets to the movies. Funniest *unusable* answer gets a kowtow: "Oh, Great Innappropriate Jokester, we honor you. Now stop it."

2. Start a file of jokes and comic strip clippings.

3. Also on the coffee room bulletin board, post questions like, "How many ever gift-wrapped something you received as a gift, and gave it away again? Put check-mark here." Use the ones that get lots of check-marks in your next presentation. Be sure to acknowledge the contributors (with permission).

You've just learned some ways in which humor can create a sense of community in your learning environment. Use them, and watch the energy rise beyond what you ever thought possible for a subject like, say, "Claims Form Updates." Remember, if your listeners are involved, you're succeeding! *Insist* on enjoying their involvement; they will only give you more. And they will accept your efforts at correction, guidance, and redirection with far better grace.

Time now to look at some ways in which humor, creativity, and play can be used to enlist two of the brain's most-used memory aids. Turn the page, Fearless One, and find out all about. . .

relevancy and visual memory— two powerful mnemonics

YOU NOW KNOW that the brain is more like a sieve than a sponge—that it lets go of far more information than it keeps—and that Brain-Compatible Learning techniques are essentially those that make information too "big" to fit through the "holes." Again, these techniques do this by presenting information in ways that speak to the brain's survival-based wiring—essentially telling the learner's brain that our information will *keep the learner alive*. Two techniques that make information positively "huge" are:

1. Making information personally relevant

2. Presenting information visually

Let's look at these two mnemonics in turn, and then see fun ways we can make them work for us.

Personal Relevancy

Why are so many high school students apparently unable to memorize the multiplication tables or the names of fifty state capitols, yet easily able to recall the lyrics to innumerable pop songs? Of course, **rhyme, rhythm,** and **music** play a big role. First and foremost, however, the lyrics are relevant to their personal lives and concerns.

See Chap 2

See Chap 2

Relevancy essentially refers to **intrinsic motivation** or the way we *personally connect* with information, or give it meaning to ourselves. You have no doubt noticed how you find a story more compelling when you can see parallels in it to your own life. In the same way, your learners will respond better when an example or problem you use easily relates back to their own experiences. It has been colorfully observed that we consider information "relevant"—intrinsically motivating—only when we feel it will do one or more of three things:

1. Increase our gain

2. Ease our pain

3. Entertain

These three things may not necessarily keep us alive, but they could certainly be said to optimize our chances of survival—or at least our quality of life! Accordingly, the brain codes relevant information as important. Bingo—it is now too big to get through the holes in the sieve!

The first two things—more gain and less pain—tend to get the highest payoff in terms of permanent behavior change, since these are the most primal of our needs, shared even with one-celled organisms. So the question you should constantly ask while designing and delivering your presentations is, *"How will this information accomplish either for my listeners?"* Maybe the skills you are teaching will put your learners in the top 2 percent of people in their department, making them serious candidates for interesting projects and future career advancement (more gain). Maybe they will result in less aggravation from customers, employees, peers, or supervisors, or can also be used to smooth their relationships with their spouse or kids (less pain). Whatever the benefits, make sure your listeners know about them! They will respond by remembering your material better.

> **"My greatest discovery of all was discovering what people want to use."**
> Thomas Edison, inventor and great respecter of relevancy

A very quick way to make your curriculum feel relevant to your learners is by, whenever possible, *enlisting their involvement in determining course content.* This will give them an immediate sense of shared ownership, making them far more willing to partner with you throughout the learning process. Here is a technique I have found to work well in sharing ownership:

Presentation Technique: "Pulse-Taking" Flip Chart

This is another time-honored tradition, and one you should always use if only because you may find out that your learners have questions you weren't planning to address! (If so, this is a good thing for you to discover. If not, they will still know they had some say in determining their own learning.)

WHAT TO DO

1. At the beginning of any program, ask your learners what they hope to get out of the training experience. Write all responses on a flip chart. If anyone mentions a goal that is even slightly humorous, be sure to laugh and enthusiastically write it down. This will make everyone sit up a little straighter and become more involved.

2. If no one says anything funny, try to come up with something yourself. Make it something you know they want. For example, if there are refreshments at the back of the training room, you can always use the old standby, "Does anyone hope to get their fill of fattening Danish pastry today?" This will always get a few raised hands and a laugh (a bigger one if you soberly write "Danish pastry" on the flip chart). Often learners will take your cue and raise their hands to suggest other gag items for the list. As long as their humor isn't inappropriate (see Chapter 10), always say, "Of *course* you want that; you'd be a fool not to," or some such, and enthusiastically include it on the chart. When the list is finished, stand back, wave a hand in its direction, and say: "I promise that you will get...well...*many* of these things from this program." This will get a very respectable laugh from your now-energized learners.

3. Post the list on one wall for the duration of the module. Mentally use it as a guide as you deliver your curriculum.

4. About ten minutes before the end of each module ask, "How many goals have we fulfilled?" Put big check marks beside the ones that have been met. This will allow the learners who stated the goals to feel validated, while giving everyone else the intrinsic motivation of **immediate success**.

See
Chap 2

TIPS

❖ Make no mistake: *Your objective here is to have every serious question checked off by the end of training!* If you do not make a conscientious effort to do so, the whole exercise will look like a snow job to your learners, and this will hurt your credibility. If by the end of a module you find you were not able to answer all their questions, try at least to direct them to wherever they can find the answers on their own. When you take this much trouble on their behalf, they will be willing to accept something less than perfection.

❖ Notice that the humorous item noted above (the Danish pastry) is *positive* in nature. Remember what we said in Chapter 4: Positivity and negativity seem to have very different effects on the brain, the former enhancing creative and cognitive thought, and the latter suppressing it. So do not use negative humor like, "How many just wanted to get out of work today?" or "How many just want to get your professional development credits out of the way?"

Note: Two other techniques in this book—Quirky Show-of-Hands Questions (Chapter 6) and Goal Assessment Charts (Chapter 9)—also help to give learners a sense of shared ownership.

And now for a superb way to create relevancy: **Build in challenge.** See Chap 2

Learner Activity: Do It Without Instructions

This activity is based on brain research suggesting that humans learn "declarative knowledge" (knowledge that can be shared with someone else) better through trying and failing than from doing it right the first time. It is especially appropriate for teaching mechanical and technical topics; writing business letters, proposals, etc.; navigating computer programs; scripting sales calls, and a host of other easily broken-down tasks. In terms of long-term learning, the fine-tuning that happens through this process is far more valuable than a lecture ever could be. And it certainly offers opportunities for Clown Bows—Ta-da!

Peer feedback comes into play particularly well in this game: When See Chap 6 learners help each other figure out the task, everyone is involved all the time. That means that the ones who take a little longer to catch on are

See
Chap 2
not working while everyone else waits. You have created an environment that allows for the **uniqueness** of each learner's brain wiring without making any learner feel "slow."

WHAT TO DO

1. At the beginning of your learning session, let learners try accomplishing the task *without instruction*. Give them a fixed amount of time (not too much!) in which to do this.

2. Call time, and give feedback by pointing out (or if possible, asking them) the main components of the task. Did they miss any?

3. Now have them return to the task and make any adjustments they feel are necessary. Give feedback again.

4. Do this again, then again, till everyone has gotten it right. Keep feedback high throughout!

And now, what about those topics that simply have no immediate relevancy for your learners? The multiplication tables again come to mind as an admirable example (although there are many others in the business world). Sure, the information will help them sometime down the road. But in the immediate present it will not increase their gain, and it *certainly* won't ease their pain—to the contrary, in fact; it's boring and irksome. How do you make that kind of material relevant?

> **"It is the true nature of mankind to learn from mistakes, not from example."**
> Fred Hoyle, British astronomer

And here once again is where humor comes in. For, as everyone knows, it entertains!

Remember the story in Chapter 2 of the pre-flight safety announcement on Southwest Airlines? Ask yourself when was the last time you listened to one of those messages all the way through? The flight attendants on Southwest got a lot of very serious but extremely dull information across. They made it fun, and so we paid attention. But there's more to the story than that.

For centuries, public speakers have known that *when people enjoy listening to a message, they are far more likely to agree and comply with it.* Southwest Airlines may provide a shining example of this principle in action. That company uses the smallest number of employees per aircraft in its industry, yet consistently earns top awards for customer service and on-time performance. I strongly suspect this is because Southwest's staff-members enjoy a higher-than-average level of customer cooperation, due at least in part to their fun approach. *That's* intrinsic motivation!

So let's look at more ways to use humor just for plain old fun. In Chapter 6, you learned the importance of letting learners **flock** by forming learning teams. Once you've done that, you can now begin employing a *BIG* relevancy technique.

See Chap 6

COMPETITION

Competition always involves challenge, and as such represents a significant intrinsic motivator for the brain—that is, as long as it doesn't serve as a way of making people feel they don't "measure up." (To help circumvent this possibility, I often get my learners into the Ta-Da! spirit with a quick, preliminary game of "Numbers Horseshoe," described in Chapter 10.) Learning teams can compete in both peer teaching and **review** activities. This book offers a host of games that can be played competitively, like "Balloon Breaks," "Dr. Truth," and "Game Show." You will find many more in *The Big Book of Humorous Training Games,* listed in the bibliography. For now we will focus on competition itself. Here are some ways I've found to facilitate competition so that it motivates intrinsically rather than extrinsically.

See Chap 9

Presentation Technique: Awarding Scores in Competitive Activities

Scoring your learning teams on their work is probably the single most fun and motivating way to give **feedback**. The running tally lets everyone know how they're doing from moment to moment, and keeps involvement high throughout the module.

See Chap 6

WHAT TO DO

See
Chap 2

1. After creating your teams, inform them that there will be many competitions throughout the module, and at the end the winning team will receive "Fabulous Prizes." (For some reason, this always gets a laugh.) *Tip:* Don't tell them what the prizes are! It will help to keep them in **states** of curiosity and anticipation.

2. When beginning each competitive learning activity, tell the teams how many points they will win by fulfilling various requirements of the game. The number of points you give for any activity is entirely up to you—but keep in mind what it is you're trying to encourage! As an example, in team presentations I always give *one* point for anything they do that gets a laugh from the class, and *two* points for each curriculum item a team addresses. This is because although I want them to play with the curriculum, ultimately I want them to learn it. This scoring system ensures that my learners will put first things first.

3. During each activity, record scores privately on a pad of paper. Then, at the end of each activity, write the totals on a flip chart or whiteboard. And here's a vital tip: *Don't itemize publicly!* Don't say, for instance, "Your team got two points each for this fact, that fact, that fact, and one point each for this laugh, that laugh, and that laugh. . . ." Just say, "For facts, you got a total of ___; for laughs, a total of ___," and let it go. Otherwise, they'll nickel and dime you to death. Trust me on this one.

4. To build excitement, keep subtotaling on the flip chart or whiteboard, so that teams always know who is ahead and by how much. Tip: Don't allow too wide a spread between team scores! If "The Flying Apple Peelers" team gets, say, twenty-three points in an activity, while "The Bruce Springsteen Fan Club" team gets only nine points, you will have demotivated TBSFC. At the end of each activity, before writing totals on the flip chart or whiteboard, just

look at the scores on your notepad. Mentally add a few points to any really low scores—not enough to bring them equal to those of the other teams, but enough to keep them in the running.

5. End the day with a final activity. Announce the final scores, and write the totals with a flourish. If your teams have made up cheers (Chapter 6), invite the winning team to bellow theirs in triumph. (Note: Often this invitation will be unnecessary, as they will do so spontaneously.)

6. Hand out the "Fabulous Prizes" to the winning team, congratulate everybody, and end the module on a high note.

TIPS

❖ Although, as noted above, you should be subjective in your scoring, if any team seriously distinguishes itself in a given activity, its members will rightfully expect to receive a substantially higher score than the other teams. In fact, the other teams will also expect this. You need to give it to them.

❖ A classy way to announce the winning team is to do the final tally in ascending order. *Example:* "The Cold Call Junkies had 78 points. In this activity, they got an additional 22 points, bringing them to a grand total of... *100 points!* (Lead applause.) The Super Closers had 72 points, but won 31 points in this competition, giving them a total of. . .103 points! (Applause.) The Field Hands were trailing with 69 points, but with a big 36, leapt into first place with. . .105! (Wild applause, huge anticipation.) So now the only question remaining is: Did Soft Sell. . .with a prior score of 75 points. . .take the day? With an addition of. . .(wait for it). . .31 points, YES, Soft Sell OWNS this competition! That's right, at 106, *Soft Sell IS THE WINNING TEAM!*" (Lead uproarious applause.)

While we're on the subject of points, never delete points for errors; it has a chilling effect. Never punish failure (Ta-Da!); only reward success.

Speaking of which, it's time to examine the tremendous value of awarding bonus points.

Presentation Technique: Bonus Points!

Bonus points should always be given for creativity—and certainly for anything that gets other learners to laugh. Bonus points represent one of the best means of making your creative environment intriguing, yet safe, for your learners.

Think about it: Why did so many of my traffic school's students express such unbridled pleasure at having spent eight hours in uncomfortable high school desks hearing about stopping distances, decapitation, and the like? Not because of the instructors' dazzling stand-up routines—we may all have been comic geniuses (in most cases unrecognized), but none of our listeners could have endured that much comedic brilliance. No, it was because *they* were the ones being funny and creative. And we had lured them into the limelight with the promise of bonus points for any behavior that we (again, very subjectively) deemed "creative."

WHAT TO DO

1. When introducing the first competitive learning activity, tell the teams that besides winning the usual points for fulfilling game requirements, they will also get bonus points for laughs and creativity. A tip: Always explain bonus points humorously. Remember, humor enlists buy-in. Getting your attendees to laugh about bonus points will virtually guarantee that they'll compete enthusiastically for them. Here is a sample script; feel free to steal any and all ideas you like:

   "In each of today's exercises I will be giving five bonus points for anything I consider 'creative.' By the way, I get to define creativity however I wish. Why you ask? Because I am the Big Kahuna, of course. [Note: People love this line, for some reason, as long as you say it with conviction.] I will also give one, two, or three points for *anything* you do that gets a laugh. The One-Point laugh sounds something like this: 'Mm-hm-hm.' Two-Point laughs are when someone opens their mouth and actual sound comes out, much like this: 'Ha ha.' And Three-Point laughs are outright guffaws, *accompanied by applause.* Got it? Okay. [Note: I do in fact get at least one "Three-Pointer" in almost every one of my classes. But early in the program this possibility seems outlandish—and therefore highly intriguing—to my learners. The very suggestion that they may accomplish such a feat opens up the possibility that anything truly might happen in this class, and that is exciting. And of course, when a team or individual *does* get a Three-Pointer, their exhilaration knows no bounds.] By the way, to earn these points, your laughs have to come from... *the other teams!* That's right, folks, no beefing up your score by laughing uproariously at your own jokes. It's been tried. I'm not stupid, you know...."

2. In the very first activity, make a point of awarding bonus points for any attempts to do things differently, no matter how low-key or timid! Say something like: "Team #3, 'The Worker Safety Pins,' gets five bonus points for actually *holding up a pair of glasses* as they discussed Physical Handicaps. Brilliant! Pure Shakespeare. My eyes were wet...."

The other teams will catch on at once. In the next exercise, they will try more unusual ways of communicating. They'll go a little further in the next exercise, then a little further...and before you know it they'll be amazing themselves and their colleagues with their risk-taking and originality—all the while creating some highly memorable learning experiences. Perhaps most importantly, in the process they'll touch a youthful, fun-loving part of their nature they have almost forgotten existed. As the day progresses, you will see them virtually falling in love with themselves. Believe me, this is a real high when it happens, both for them and for you.

I've always believed this heightened self-appreciation was the sole reason attendees at our Traffic Violator School so often asked, "Would I have to get another ticket to come back here?" (Boy, did we come to expect that joke! Of course, we never let on we'd heard it before.) Meanwhile, did they learn the material? *Par excellence.*

IMPORTANT TIP YOU MIGHT NOT THINK ABOUT
Give bonus points for orderly behavior as well as good performance. Yes, crowd control is an important part of Creative Learning. For instance, you should give five points to the first entire team to come to order when you call for attention, four to the second team to pull itself together, and so on. You can do the same to encourage teams to get back from breaks on time. For more on crowd control, see Chapter 10.

And now the moment has come to look carefully at an extremely serious aspect of learner competition.

FABULOUS PRIZES!

See
Chap 2 You'd think this part would be the no-brainer, right? After all, the module is nearly over, they've done their work, and all that's left now is **celebration**—how hard can that be?

And the answer is: Not very. Still, the way you select and use prizes is important, in that it can spell the difference between motivating and demotivating your learners. So let's call this issue a "semi-brainer"—it's not mysterious, but you do need to think about it.

In a nutshell, *demotivating* prizes include:

1. Those given only for good performance

2. Those with market value

Let's look at each in turn.

PRIZES FOR GOOD PERFORMANCE. In consulting with the training department of one Fortune 500 company, I one day noticed that the trainers gave prizes only to those learners who got answers right. Predictably, some learners had quickly amassed mountains of prizes, while others sat with few or none. This created a powerful visual statement of who was "smart" and who was "slow." Meanwhile, the very act of giving prizes began to take on a good-dog-here's-your-biscuit feel. Not too surprisingly, most trainees tended to remain silent unless they knew for sure they had the correct answer, and many seldom participated at all. With the best intentions in the world, these trainers had created a demotivating environment.

We changed the policy to "Good Guesses Win Good Stuff," wherein any really thoughtful contribution in class—even if it missed the point completely—was rewarded. Almost immediately, things perked up; learners began to respond, to take risks, to volunteer for role-plays, to ask probing questions that showed they were thinking about the material. In short, they began to take ownership of their learning!

I have seen this same scenario played out time and again. For this reason, I issue this directive with supreme confidence: *Give your Fabulous Prizes to at least as many of those who make GOOD TRIES as those who answer questions correctly.*

(This, by the way, is also why I give bonus points: to lift people out of their inhibitions and encourage them to bravely wrestle with the curriculum.)

And now let's look at the other demotivator.

MARKET-VALUE PRIZES. In many cases, items like money, bonuses, promotions, parking spaces, or even certificates of achievement—things writer Alfie Kohn has called "bribes"—have actually been shown to be brain antagonistic. Why? Because they tend to cheapen the experience of accomplishment by shifting focus to material gain.

Now, please don't misunderstand me! I am not saying that people do not need to be financially rewarded for good work on the job—this is known as making a living. What I am saying is that *in the learning environment,* market-value rewards tend to be counter-productive, creating a game of escalating expectations that, ultimately, you won't win. Always remember: The brain is wired with its own intrinsic motivators, which are what virtually every technique in this book primarily seeks to enlist. As you saw in Chapter 2, these include **immediate success** ("What do you know, I did it!"); **satisfaction** ("I'm always good at tasks like this"); **novelty** ("Ooh, how interesting!"); **role model motivation** ("I want to do it as well as she did"); and **celebration** ("Let's hear it for our side"). Key point: Your "Fabulous Prizes" should always be fun, symbolic gestures of celebration, *not* patronizing rewards for good behavior.

The best Fabulous Prizes are—surprise, surprise—humorous! Here is a partial list of inexpensive items that I have found to work well for the purpose. All of these little goodies seem to motivate learners astonishingly well, creating a feeling of competition while maintaining perspective. . . .

PARTIAL LIST OF APPROPRIATE FABULOUS PRIZES

❖ Tootsie Pops,® Pixie Stix,® or any other candies kids typically play with as well as eat.

❖ Gag certificates that say things like "Most Inquiring Mind" or "Biggest Risk-Taker." Make up more of your own; just remember to make them positive in nature, not derogatory.

❖ Funny memo and "sticky" pads (obtainable at many business and stationery stores).

❖ Small toys like Slinkies,® Silly Putty,® koosh balls, bubble-makers, and more. (All of these, and other items like them, can be found in novelty, party, or magic stores. They are perhaps most easily obtainable through Trainer's Warehouse.[1])

A CAUTIONARY TIP

As with points, people can also become quite inflamed about prizes. This is actually the reason I love the term "Fabulous": When they hear it, my learners always laugh cynically—then immediately begin competing with rabid fervor! Besides working hard at their exercises, they also challenge every score, demand recounts, claim bonus points for this innovation or that, and generally act like a bunch of clamorous kids. But that's really quite lovely, since at one point in the proceedings it forces me to issue this severe reprimand: "Hey, people! You know those Fabulous Prizes I mentioned? Well, *THEY'RE NOT REALLY THAT FABULOUS!*"

This always gets a thunderous laugh as my intelligent learners realize they knew this all along, and were working like berserkers just the same. And at this point they seem to make an unconscious decision to keep right on doing so—suddenly they see that this learning stuff is fun in and of itself. As a teacher, you've just got to love that!

> **"To learn, you must want to be taught."**
> Proverbs 12:1

Reflection Section

What are some ways your own curriculum is personally relevant to your learners? How does the material increase their gain, ease their pain, or entertain? (Remember: If the only ways are through money or job security, they are *extrinsically* motivating, and you may want to examine your presentation more closely!)

....

....

....

....

....

....

....

....

We've seen some new ways to infuse our communications with relevancy. Now let's look at ways we can use the second mnemonic.

Visual Memory

In her book, *What I Saw at the Revolution,* Peggy Noonan relates how Michael Deaver, Press Secretary to Ronald Reagan, once told Presidential assistant Richard Darman: "Listen, Dick, I don't care what else you do, but make sure you do this: Get that [Reagan's] face on television. This is a face that when a baby sees it, the baby smiles."[2]

A recognized innovator in public relations, Deaver made great use of visual memory. He regularly created photo ops placing Reagan in settings that both flattered the President *and* made for "good TV" (read: created images television producers couldn't resist using). Bill Moyers tells how, on a day that Reagan signed a bill unfavorable to blue-collar workers, Deaver arranged a photo op for the press in which the President was shown hoisting a beer with patrons at a working class bar. Leslie Stahl, who reported the bill signing on the nightly news, only later realized that the American working-class public had registered little concern over her story, so potent were the visual images that accompanied it.[3]

Most veteran trainers are familiar with the term "multimodal," which refers to the various preferred learning styles (sometimes called sensory systems) that differentiate us as individuals. Stated briefly, it is known that some of us remember better by seeing the information, others by hearing it, and still others by interacting with it. It is true that optimally effective communication addresses all three modalities. Still, just as Michael Deaver realized, *everyone remembers pictures best.* Replicated studies have shown that long-term recall of visual imagery is between 85 percent to 99 percent accurate! In other words, if we see it, there's an excellent likelihood we'll remember it. (Ever say, "I'm no good with names, but I never forget a face?" There you go.) The brain probably figures that paying attention to visuals will *keep us alive* because visuals are tangible—they could eat us, or vice versa. Words or thoughts can't do that.

So let's look at this important phenomenon more closely. First, we know that the brain can register *over 36,000 visual images per hour*—that's a lot of learning! Second, most of these images are received nonconsciously—and as you read in Chapter 2, **nonconscious** learning is powerful learning. Apparently one picture is worth a thousand words!

There are many ways to use visuals as effective learning devices. You may already be making use of overheads, PowerPoint presentations, and videos. That's good, as long as they are in harmony with your live communication (technology will never replace human interaction). Some more light-hearted ways to use visuals are through posters, mind maps, and—are you ready?—jokes! Let's take these one by one.

POSTERS

In Chapter 5, you saw four examples of written **affirmations**. Adding visuals to the words can greatly increase the impact of the messages. Here are examples of how these posters might look:

❖ *"Student Exchanges* between departments work." (Figure 7-1)

❖ "My *Difficult* Person might just be a *Different* Person." (Figure 7-2)

❖ "I can verbally *ask,* and vocally *tell."* (Figure 7-3)

❖ *"Actively listen,* and the world will beat a path to your door." (Figure 7-4)

FIGURE 7-1. Student Exchanges between deparments work.

FIGURE 7-2. My Difficult Person might just be a Different Person.

FIGURE 7–3. I can verbally ask, and vocally tell.

FIGURE 7–4. Actively listen, and the world will beat a path to your door.

All your posters can easily include simple illustrations—done by you! Just so you know, I drew the ones on the preceding pages. (No applause, please, you'll only embarrass me.) If you are not already familiar with *your* innate ability to draw, it is time to become so. The fact is that everybody can draw. These days many books exist especially for teachers and trainers, showing how to do quick, good-looking illustrations for posters, flip charts, etc. For a listing of some of these, see the bibliography. One book I recommend in particular, which will serve more than one purpose for you, is *Mapping Inner Space: Learning and Teaching Visual Mapping*, by Nancy Margulies.[4] It contains several pages showing you how to draw common objects for use in mind maps. And if you don't yet know about mind maps, you should—they represent another, particularly potent learning tool.

In fact, I know what: Let's look at mind maps now! (Smooth transition, huh? Thank you, I thought so.)

MIND MAPS

The time-honored tradition of writing notes in linear, outline format uses only a small part of the brain's natural processing style. The brain works both linearly and associatively: Dendritic branchings do go from neuron to neuron, but each neuron may also connect three-dimensionally with dozens, hundreds, and even thousands of others in what BCL expert Eric Jensen calls a "rain forest" or "jungle matrix" of understanding. As you now know, the brain also tends to think in pictures rather than words. This is where mind maps come in. You could say that, by using both pictures and multiple associations, mind maps speak the brain's language.

Mind maps allow you (and your learners) to take notes creatively and connectedly. The steps are simple:

1. Place the main topic in the center of your paper.

2. Radiate key subtopics outward on curved branches.

3. Add details to the branches.

4. Add art.

You can use mind maps to show the outline of your program, or have your learners draw their own, adding to them as your program progresses. For an example of a mind map, see Figure 7-5.

JOKES

How do jokes qualify as visuals, you ask? Think of the joke, "He's so uptight he got his elbows pierced so he could wear cuff links in the summer." For this to be actually funny, you have to get a *mental picture* of the guy with the cuff links impaling his elbows. The advertising world is rife with hilarious stories about corporations that have unwittingly created unsavory mental pictures when introducing their products to other cultures:

❖ In China, the name Coca-Cola was reportedly first submitted as "Ke-kou-ke-la," which unfortunately means either "bite the wax tadpole" or "a female horse stuffed with wax," depending on one's dialect. (It turns out that Coca-Cola's own name was best! In Chinese, "Coca" means "tasty" and "Cola" means "fun" or "makes you happy," so the overall meaning becomes something like "happiness in the mouth." Who knew?)

❖ In Taiwan, Pepsi's slogan, "Come alive with the Pepsi Generation," apparently translated to: "Pepsi will bring your ancestors back from the dead," a concept bound to inspire some ambivalence.

❖ In Chinese, KFC's "finger-lickin' good" can be read: "Eat your fingers off." Yum!

Comedy writer Gene Peret has said that humor is "largely graphic." I say that to all intents and purposes, he's right. Although I still maintain that you don't have to tell jokes to express your natural sense of humor, the fact remains that if you *do* like telling them you can use them to good advantage. If you feel the need to build your skill in this area, visit Chapter 11.

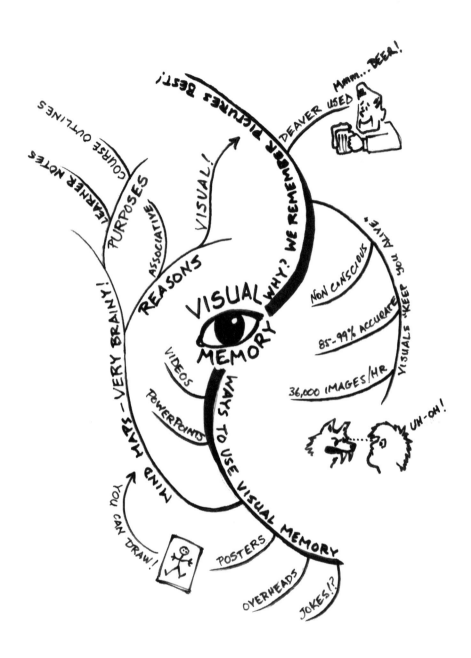

FIGURE 7-5. Example of a mind map.

Reflection Section

If you thought you could *quickly* learn to draw better than you do, would you put in the time? Can you outline your next program using a mind map rather than an outline form? Heard any good jokes lately? What are some other ways you could employ more visuals in your programs?

....

....

....

....

....

....

....

....

....

....

Some Next Steps

1. Look over your programs, and see if you can think of ways the information therein can help your learners in their personal lives as well as their jobs.

2. Think of any *positive* reasons your learners might want to attend your program, which have nothing to do with the curriculum. Use these to bring humor to your "Pulse-Taking Flip Chart."

3. Look through your curriculum to find any simple mechanical or technical skills that your learners can practice without instruction.

4. If necessary, get one of the drawing books listed in the bibliography, and create some affirmation posters.

5. Get Nancy Margulies' *Mapping Inner Space.* Create a mind map of your next program. Post it, work from it, and have learners copy (and add to) it.

6. Go through your now-growing Joke-and-Cartoon file, and find any pieces of humor that are relevant to a topic you're currently presenting. Insert the jokes into your oral presentation, or make overheads of the cartoons. Observe the response.

You have just looked at some ways to enlist the powerful mnemonics of relevancy and visual communication. We are about to move on to a process that is indispensable to learning. Since this one is so vital, why not take a moment right now to boost that BDNF in your brain with some quick aerobics, or maybe a couple of Cross Laterals. . . . Oh wait, you don't know what BDNF and Cross Laterals are yet. Okay, just do the aerobics, and then high-tail it over to the next chapter to find out all about. . .

engaging

emotion

IN THIS CHAPTER:

* ❖ The critical role of emotions in thinking

* ❖ Why it is useful to acknowledge your negative emotions

* ❖ The difference your enthusiasm can spell for your learners

* ❖ "Pacing," and why you should do it (a lot)

* ❖ Why affirmations work

* ❖ The effects of music on the brain

* ❖ *Loads of tricks and techniques*

WRITER DANIEL GOLEMAN recounts a fascinating and sad tale of a man he calls Elliot.[1] Surgery had removed a tumor from Elliot's brain, but had also severed the ties between his neocortex and the so-called emotional brain (the midbrain). After the operation, his friends noticed that he was somehow "no longer Elliot." Although he was intellectually as capable as ever, his decision-making had become computer-like. He could weigh the pros and cons of any choice, but could not give *emotional value* to either side. As a result, even the most insignificant decision-making was a time-consuming task, as he constantly got mired in the most minor details. In addition, he no longer seemed to learn from experience. Unable to attach emotions like shame, triumph, fear, or satisfaction to any in-cident in his life, he had no "gut" feeling about either repeating or avoiding it. His life began to fall apart. Once a successful corporate lawyer, he now could not hold onto a job. Unable to have a satisfying relationship anymore, his wife left him. He lost his savings in a series of unwise investments.

> **"Emotion drives attention, and attention drives learning."**
> Robert Sylwester, author,
> *A Biological Brain in a Cultural Classroom*

This tragic story tells us much about the supposedly separate phe-nomena of emotions and thinking. In actual fact, without emotional involvement learning is severely limited. More than perhaps anything else, it is through emotions that our brains "code" information as important and meaningful. The brain is wired to attend first to information with emotional content; indeed, the stronger the emotion, the more meaning. Our emotions:

❖ Help us learn information faster

❖ Help us recall information better

❖ Make information feel "real" (we believe what we feel)

❖ Help us make better quality decisions about information (integrating logic with values)

The word "emotion" derives from the Latin *emovere*: to move outward. The ancients believed that emotions lead to the impulse to act. And as it happens, today's neuroscientists agree. Literally speaking, emotions are nothing more than chemical releases. (Pretty unemotional description, huh?) Goleman gives examples of how emotions create physical responses that then influence our actions:

❖ **Joy**, in which all human beings experience *increased activity in the midbrain,* inhibiting the release of distress hormones, and generally resting the body while increasing available energy.

❖ **Fear**, in which the *body freezes* momentarily while the mind focuses on the perceived threat, the *brain releases stress hormones,* and *blood flows to the larger skeletal muscles* preparatory to fleeing.

❖ **Surprise**, in which, among other things, the *eyebrows lift,* allowing more light to strike the retina and more visual information to be received.

❖ **Anger**, in which *heart rate increases, fight-or-flee hormones are released,* and *blood flows to the hands,* better enabling us to strike.

❖ **Sadness**, in which the *body's metabolism slows,* forcing us to take the added rest we need to reflect on, and heal from, loss.

❖ **Disgust**, in which the *nose wrinkles* in an apparent attempt to close out noxious scents.

At this point, you may be thinking, "Hey, I feel more than just six things!" And you'd be right. **States**, like frustration, anticipation, confidence, and more, are sometimes called secondary emotions. They stem from the primary emotions, and, like emotions, are expressed similarly from person to person. The point here is that *any of the emotions—if not too intense—can greatly further the learning process.* That means we as teachers must welcome emotional expression in our classrooms.

See Chap 2

Stop right here! Is your nose by any chance wrinkling in an attempt to keep out noxious scents (see "Disgust," above)? Are phrases like "Encounter Session," "Playing Mommy," and "Touchy-Feelie" flooding your mind? Well, great! You just watched your brain use a well-trammeled neural pathway. Wasn't that interesting?

Seriously, we've all heard of those learning theories, particularly popular in the 1970s, that mandated a sort of Peace-and-Love atmosphere in the classroom. Admittedly, these theories yielded mixed fruits. I myself have a friend who in the 1970s attended high school in—yes, okay—California. She learned a lot about "self-expression" and "sensitivity in interpersonal relations." Meanwhile (and she's the first to admit this) her spelling remains absolutely atrocious to this day. So let's be clear: I do not advocate turning your learning environment into an encounter session. I simply seek to show that your learners will remember far more of your curriculum if you present it in ways that engage their emotions.

In my experience, dealing appropriately with emotions involves three steps:

1. Reading our own emotions accurately

2. Showing acceptance of other people's emotions

3. Managing the emotional climate, so to speak.

Let's take these one by one.

Step 1: "Reading" Ourselves Accurately

This is the obvious first step—to recognize and accept our own emotional responses. And it's no easy task for some!

In particular, many of us have learned to suppress some of the negative emotions listed above, like anger, fear, and sadness, as if they were *ipso facto* bad. Yet these emotions are quite valid and appropriate in the right contexts. I don't suggest we abandon ourselves to them—certainly in social interactions we often need to weigh unregulated self-expression against group harmony. But such reserve is neither required nor healthy in our more intimate relationships. Everyone would agree that the great joy of intimacy is the freedom to express one's deeper, if not always nicer, feelings to another person; yet what many of us seem to forget is

"Know thyself."

Inscription at the
Delphic oracle

that the one person we are most intimate with is ourselves! Many of us seek to deny, even in the privacy of our own hearts, that we feel any negative emotions at all!

Unfortunately, in refusing to acknowledge our "bad" thoughts, we are immediately put at their mercy. For the fact is that unacknowledged emotions don't go away. They only go underground, where they await their opportunity to rise, Phoenix-like, and when we least expect it, jump out to bite us on the derriere. Suddenly we find ourselves treating a listener's error, thoughtlessness, or ignorance as if it was malice preconceived. We snap out an answer if they miss a key point they should have written down with alacrity; we add the tiniest whiff of sarcasm if they come across as "confrontational"; we ignore a question that seems to us to be intentionally specious.

What is lost in such interactions? Trust. And to coin a phrase, when trust goes out the door, **threat** flies in the window.

See
Chap 5

So the order of the day is emphatically: "Know thyself." But again, how?

Good news! Back in Chapter 4, you started working on your HQ. If you think about it, you may find that this work had the added effect of raising your comfort level with your emotions. Why? Because it *diluted the power of your Inner Censor*. And whether you knew it or not, this had a traveling effect: Your brain figured that if the *Ta-Da!* principle works for ideas, it must also work for emotions. In other words, as it learned tolerance for untested ideas, it also learned tolerance for risky emotions, making it safer for you to acknowledge them to yourself.

If my experience is anything to go by, emotions are much like teenagers. When met with intolerance, they become withdrawn and sullen. Given acceptance, they are more open and authentic, and generally far more tractable. (The only difference between emotions and teenagers, I suppose, is that emotions never raid your refrigerator or put their feet on the furniture, but let's let that go.) This gives you one more excellent reason to develop your natural sense of humor—to get comfortable with your emotions, thereby gaining greater understanding of them. Know thyself!

Step 2: Accepting the Emotions of Others

More good news: As you learn to remove the stigma of "wrongness" from your emotions, you will find you can't help but remove it from your learners'. My own experience with Creative Learning has been that my learners not only express more emotion while wrestling with the topic at hand, but also handle their emotions better. Not only that, they also handle each other's better. (Amazing what a good hammerlock can do—*just joking!*) It seems that in successfully controlling our Inner Censors, my learners and I create for ourselves a rare spirit of tolerance and community, in which even negative emotions can be expressed and dealt with constructively. We are then free to engage emotion in our learning, making the experience far more powerful. You can do the same in your own work.

> **"The more open we are to our own emotions, the more skilled we will be in reading feelings."**
>
> Daniel Goleman,
> emotional intelligence guru

Step 3: Emotional Management

Remember also that emotions are contagious. Indeed, we seem to be programmed that way. From infancy, simply looking at a smiling or angry face causes our own facial muscles to change to reflect that mood. Studies have shown that the emotions of relatively expressive people will get "picked up" by people who are less so.[2] This is important news for communicators of all kinds, for it means that *you as leader can help to manage your listeners' emotions by expressing appropriate ones yourself.*

> **"Leadership is practiced not so much in words as in attitude and actions."**
>
> Harold Geneen, business legend

Without implying that their inappropriate emotions are "bad," you can help to replace them with others that will be both more enjoyable and useful to everyone concerned. To do this, you need to develop and call upon three skills:

1. Your own personal enthusiasm

2. Your ability with synchrony

3. Your skill with "mood lifters"

Let's take these one by one:

PERSONAL ENTHUSIASM

Since you are reading this book, I feel safe in assuming that you're enthusiastic about teaching. And here is yet another reason for you to work on your performance skills, as recommended throughout this book—to help you to better *express* your enthusiasm, thereby transmitting it more effectively to your learners. How about a few more smiles? The occasional audible laugh? Go nuts: Raise an eyebrow sometimes. Make what in the theatre we call "emotional noises"— a small groan when you lose your place in your notes, a pleased "Hmm!" when a learner gets point, a bemused "Ah" when they make a good argument in a discussion.

> **"Nothing great was ever achieved without enthusiasm."**
> **Ralph Waldo Emerson,**
> **nineteenth-century writer**

Note: I do *not* suggest that you fake this stuff, but only that you cultivate your natural aptitude with it! Recognize that all really first-rate professional speakers work on their comfort with spontaneous expressions of emotion. That's because it's one of the single best ways to engage listeners. It is for this reason that I so highly recommend theatre improvisation for any teacher, trainer, or speaker. Theatre improv is more fun than a body's got a right to, and the training loosens you up and "naturalizes" you, making you a more spontaneous communicator overall. In fact, I know what: Let's play an improv game now!

Trainer Practice: "It's Tuesday"

This game allows you and your colleagues to practice expressing yourselves with energy and enthusiasm. The idea in this game is to "push the envelope"—overplay your enthusiasm, possibly to the point of silliness—so that you will feel comfortable expressing appropriate levels of enthusiasm in a natural way. You can play this game with a group of people, who stand in two parallel lines facing each other. You can also play with a single partner.

WHAT TO DO

1. Decide which line (or individual) is A and which is B.

2. An A goes first. She looks at the B facing her, and says something innocuous like, "It's Tuesday," "It looks like rain," "It's three o'clock," "I forgot my watch," or some such.

3. The B person must now answer in some way that gives great importance to the A's statement. Examples: "Tuesday? Fantastic! That means the World Cup is on TV," or "Wonderful—I can finally pick up my car from the shop!" "Rain! Thank heaven the dry spell is over," or "Oh good, I *love* the smell of rain!" Remember the second rule of creativity in Chapter 4: Don't be original. When you are the respondent, don't try to come up with a brilliant, witty answer. Just make it enthusiastic. (*Tip:* Go for "authenticity" rather than volume. Often this will result in a laugh—always fun when it happens, even if it's not the objective here.)

4. Now switch off, with the Bs supplying the innocuous statements, and the A's giving significance to them.

DEBRIEF

❖ How did it feel to overplay enthusiasm? How much of a stretch was it for you?

❖ If it was extremely difficult or made you highly uncomfortable, why do you think this was?

❖ Do you teach any topic so uninspiring that you cannot feel enthusiasm about it? Are there any issues surrounding the topic that you *can* feel enthusiastic about? (For example, learning a long list of text codes is boring, but once learned, you can breeze through your work far more efficiently.)

❖ When would your enthusiasm make a difference to your learners? (Possible answers: When they've done a good job [or at least made a good try] at something; when you introduce a learning activity you want them be excited about; *definitely* when they've done anything funny or creative.)

SYNCHRONY

Ever notice how, even at a distance, you can tell whether two people are getting along or not? They may not smile or in any other way look particularly happy, yet it's somehow clear they are comfortable in the situation and with each other. This is largely because they are using synchrony as they talk. One person might lean forward, and within about sixty seconds the other will also lean in. One might sit back, and after a moment the other will do likewise. In a restaurant, both might have their elbows on the table, or on their knees. We've all seen this: One person talking and nodding emphatically, the other one listening, and...well, you get the picture. Synchrony can be as subtle as two people wagging a toe or even breathing in the same rhythm! Psychologists alternately call this universal behavior "mirroring," "blending" or "pacing." Synchrony is all around you, and great fun to watch. So start watching for it. Then consider this.

Most of us tend to instinctively employ synchrony only with those with whom we feel we are "on the same wavelength." However, it has been found that people with high emotional sensitivity—easily-triggered autonomic nervous systems—employ it more often. This sends a powerful, nonconscious message of "I'm with you," which in turn *tends to make others feel more comfortable in their presence.* It's no mystery why politicians, beauty pageant contestants, and other "popularity pros" work to exercise their synchrony muscle. Luckily for us all, it's an easy muscle to develop; in fact, one could call this a no-brainer. Here's how to do it:

Trainer Practice: "I'm With You"

WHAT TO DO

In your daily interactions, start noticing not just what other people are saying to you, but the way they are saying it. How are they holding their bodies—spread out (feet apart, arms akimbo, etc.) or pulled in? Are their heads tilted a bit to one side? Do they make lots of eye contact, or relatively little? Are they folding their arms tightly, or waving their hands as they speak? Are they smiling? Looking serious? Looking bland? Also, how loudly do they speak? How quickly? The point is, whatever your partner does physically—as long as it's not inappropriate—is something you can emulate to make them feel more comfortable around you.

DEBRIEF

And now for some concerns that many people feel about using this unconscious behavior consciously:

❖ *Concern #1:* Avoid making judgments about what is "inappropriate"! Many people instinctively feel, for example, there is a *right* amount of eye-contact, vocal volume, physical space, and so on. This is not so. Check it out, if you don't believe me: There is no mention in any of the Holy Books about how close thou shalt stand, how loudly thou shalt talk, nor how much time thou shalt spend looking at someone. These things are purely a matter of preference (culturally influenced, usually), and as such are not open to criticism.

❖ *Concern #2:* Don't worry about your partner "catching" you pacing them. They won't if you keep it subtle. This is done in two ways.

1. Don't pace any behavior immediately. (Remember, we usually fall into synchrony within about a minute.)

2. Mirror, don't mimic. If they fold their arms, you can fold your hands, cross your arms, or do something else that's similar. *Key point:* Pacing usually happens at the nonconscious level. When you use it consciously, do so subtly.

❖ *Concern #3:* Definitely don't worry about being a "phony." Remember, as a card-carrying member of the human race you already *do* pace people every day—people you like. Professional communicators just carry it one step further: They pace those they don't like so much!

❖ *Concern #4:* And don't worry that pacing people you don't like makes you "manipulative." The fact is that pacing is no more manipulative than wearing a suit to work instead of your Speedo bathing suit. You do it simply because it makes people more comfortable around you. But there's one more reason to pace. Think of the maxim "Fake it till you make it." Ever wish to high heaven you could find *some* sort of common ground with a particularly exasperating person? So behave as if you already have: Pace that person! Usually you will find that you actually start to feel the commonality your body is demonstrating. In effect, your brain has believed what your body told it: that you're okay with this person. Congratulations—you've just manipulated yourself!

A final word: Synchrony is a highly developed etiquette skill in certain cultures, perhaps most notably in Asia. In Thailand, for instance, where dinner tables are often set low, anyone excusing themselves will usually stand up, bend over, and leave the room at a sort of half-mast, straightening up only once they are out the door. This is essentially pacing; they are remaining at a height relative to their floor-seated dinner partners. Studies in classroom environments have shown that the closer the synchrony between teacher and student, the more friendly, enthusiastic, interested, and relaxed participants feel working together.

I frankly call pacing a "99 percenter." That's because 99 percent of the times that I've had difficulty connecting with a person, this subtle technique alone has made a noticeable, sometimes astonishing, improvement in our relationship. Everyone who has mastered pacing has their own miracle stories to tell. Get some for yourself.

> **"Do not do unto others what you would have them do unto you: They may not have the same tastes."**
>
> George Bernard Shaw, the ultimate Shavian

MOOD LIFTERS

In Chapter 5 you saw that moderate amounts of negative stress, such as a little anxiety increasing motivation to do well on tests, can enhance learning. Still, as you saw in Chapter 4, it is the positive emotions that allow us to think with the greatest flexibly and complexity—to think most creatively. So we teachers shouldn't ignore some of the tried-and-true techniques for raising human spirits that have existed for centuries. Many of these are quite appropriate to the learning environment, helping to create what is called "hypomania," the state of mild elation generally found present in artists of all kinds as they do their work. Here are three that work particularly well in a learning setting: aerobics, treats, and music.

Learner Activity: Aerobic Exercise

Yep, it's not just for Californians anymore! If aerobic exercise is considered one of the more effective strategies against mild clinical depression, think what it can do for your learners. Besides, neuroscientists have discovered that exercise releases BDNF, a neurotrophic factor that boosts the ability of neurons to communicate with each other. So consider starting morning and afternoon learning modules with some bending, stretching, arm swinging, etc.

See
Chap 5

TIPS

❖ A good way to let learners feel **choice** in this activity is to have each team delegate a member to lead exercises they prefer. Be sure to ask any Jazzercise aficionados to go easy on their colleagues!

❖ Play music in the background during exercises (see below).

Presentation Technique: Treats

The sensual pleasures—hot baths, food, sex, etc.—are well-known mood enhancers. For our purposes here we'll stick to food, shall we? (I knew you'd agree.) So have a few nibblies around! These need not be candy and cookies; in fact, such sugary delights, as you well know, are hardly good for optimal brain function. Meanwhile, certain other foods actually enhance brain function. Fresh fruits, especially bananas, apples, oranges, and papayas, and nuts like pecans and peanuts are some of the brain's favorite forms of fuel. Sneak a few of these on your learners instead of the traditional Snickers and Danish pastries, and hear them say, "He likes it—hey, Mikey!" (Extra points for you if you got that reference.) And of course, always have water present; next to oxygen, it's the brain's all-time favorite fuel.

Presentation Technique: Music

It has been said of music that there is no faster way to create or change moods. Innumerable studies have been done on the effects of music on various living things. Although the "Mozart Effect"—the supposed way in which music magically boosts intelligence—has been vastly overstated in recent years, it seems that different genres of music do have different effects on thinking. Let's look at a few:

❖ Baroque music (1600–1760)—Handel, Vivaldi, Bach, and others—is said to be particularly conducive to creating a relaxed state of alertness, perfect for *receiving new information*. Some speakers and teachers play it at low volumes in the background before or even during lectures.

❖ Classical music (1760–1825)—Haydn, Mozart, Meyerbeer, Beethoven, and others—seems to evoke the childlike, imaginative, creative nature in listeners. Consider playing it for *brainstorming, storytelling, or whenever you want to create an "electric" moment to boost memory.*

❖ Romantic music (1825–1900)—Tchaikovsky, Brahms, Schubert, Mendelssohn, and others—creates moods of wonder, ecstasy, and strangeness. You might use it to help your learners *change negative attitudes and better bond with whatever they are learning.* It is particularly good for studying the arts (including graphics and technical writing), but can also be used for guided imagery and stories.

TIPS

❖ Many learners (including me) find music distracting during quiet moments like solitary writing.

❖ Studies exist suggesting that some rock music literally reduces physical strength and stunts plant growth! Still, I have found that rock and pop music can be quite appropriate for breaks, and also for high-octane activities during which learners are making enough noise not to be distracted by the lyrics. Here are some I like:

1. Greatest hits of the Eagles—both volumes

2. Soundtrack from *The Commitments*

3. Greatest hits of Queen (especially "We Will Rock You" and "We Are the Champions")

4. Every song Marvin Gaye ever recorded (okay, except "Sexual Healing")

5. Collections of the biggest rock hits of the 1980s

6. The *Multivolume History of Rock & Roll Radio*

7. The Beatles' "Magical Mystery Tour" album

Use this music in good health, and boogie down!
(For a listing of additional music resources, especially for teachers and trainers, consult the bibliography at the end of the book.)

Reflection Section

Explain to a colleague what you've just learned about the role of emotions in thinking. Then discuss with the colleague: How comfortable are you with your "less acceptable" emotions, like anger and fear? If your answer is "Not very," can you see any correlation between this and your effectiveness in accepting and managing such emotions in your learning environment?

....

....

....

....

....

....

....

....

....

....

....

Some Next Steps

1. Make up a list of affirmations. Use anything you like—just keep them positive and short: "No flies on us!" "This team rocks!" etc.

2. Call a local theatre school and ask about theatre improvisation classes in your area. Or look up *www.intl-theatresports.ab.ca,* and see if they have a school near you.

3. Practice consciously pacing your partner in every conversation for the next two weeks. (If they're on the phone, pace their vocal tone, volume, and speed.) Remember: mirror, don't mimic!

4. Get some fresh fruits and/or nuts, set them out in your classroom, and observe the response.

5. Get some music tapes and a portable tape deck. Bring these to your next presentation. Play the tapes as people arrive and during exercises and breaks. Observe the response.

In this chapter, I have sought to reaffirm that you need not evoke out-and-out laughter in order to lighten up your classroom. After all, the goal in Creative Learning is not screaming hilarity, but a sense of lightness and play. The enjoyable, light-touch techniques offered here will help you to engage emotions in unthreatening ways to help your learners have an *experience* with your curriculum. Truly has it been said, "Theory plus experience equals knowledge."

In the next chapter we'll look at some Creative Learning techniques specifically designed to allow the brain one thing it must have to cement learning. Read on, and see how the brain can seem just like a romantic partner when it tells you. . .

"I need my space!"

giving the brain regular breathers for enhanced learning

CHAPTER

DALE CARNEGIE once told a story of two men who were out in the forest together chopping wood. One of the men worked unceasingly, taking no breaks and stopping only briefly for lunch. The other paused numerous times throughout the day, and even took a short nap after his midday meal. By nightfall, the first man was astonished to see that the second had cut more wood than he!

"I don't understand it," he said. "Every time I looked around, you seemed to be sitting down. Yet you've accomplished more than I have. How can that be?"

His companion responded serenely: "Didn't you notice that while I was sitting down, I was sharpening my axe?"

In recent years, we have become all-too familiar with the expression "Doing More with Less." Around the world, jobs have been eliminated and budgets slashed in the cherished theory that under tightened time constraints people would "work smarter." Has this happened? According to management consultant Alan Downs, forty-hour work weeks have in many cases expanded to sixty and even eighty hours, while in the meantime we have seen a dramatic increase in stress-related illness and absenteeism and a decrease in overall quality[1]. In my own consulting work, I have certainly observed these things firsthand. I am not surprised: To think and work well, we need regular breaks to sharpen our axes.

What does this mean for teaching professionals? It means that no matter how urgently our learners need to get "up to speed," *we cannot force-feed them our curriculum.* The brain needs time to transfer information from short- to long-term memory. Brain-Compatible Learning can certainly reduce the amount of time needed—that is probably the major part of its value—but it cannot circumvent the need itself.

> **"Woe to him who teaches men faster than they can learn."**
> William J. Durant,
> American historian

So let's look at three ways the brain must pause to sharpen its axe—

1. Making meaning

2. Heightening attention

3. Reviewing information

—and learn some fun techniques that can expedite these processes.

Axe-Sharpener #1: Making Meaning

Do something right now: Read the following ten nonsense words out loud twice, then look away from the page and write them down immediately. Ready? Go!

ZIGGA FRENOL AVRIN SERROLA RIH BLUN VASSIT UNGOT RICKAB GROF

Now try it again, this time with these words:

EARTH WORM BIRD SKY SUN PLANET GALAXY UNIVERSE INFINITY GOD

How did you do with the first group? The second? I think I can guess.

When I lived in Canada, we had a saying for when things were messy or disorganized: "*That's* a real dog's breakfast, eh?" (An expressive people, the Canadians.) That's sort of what your brain says when confronted with meaningless factoids that have no relation to anything else. And, as you've just seen, the brain dumps those factoids unceremoniously!

Meaning—context—vitally impacts attention. After all, how can meaningless information *keep us alive?* Even if it's vitally important, we can't intelligently figure out what to do with it, so there's no real point in holding onto it. In short, *you will lose your learners if you fling information at them without letting their brains make meaning of it.*

> **"The distinction between fact finding and 'meaning making' is what distinguishes shallow from deep learning."**
> Colin Rose,
> accelerated learning authority

The question now becomes: How does the brain make meaning? Two ways involve seeing the Big Picture, and using productive downtime.

THE BIG PICTURE

Did you notice that, besides being intelligible to you, the second group of words in the lists above also related to each other and were arranged in a context (i.e., lowly-to-sublime)? These two things helped you to remember them better than if they had been unintelligible and random. This is what you need to do with your curriculum: present it in ways that let your learners' brains easily see *what the information means,* as well as *how each bit relates to the others.* One powerful way to do that is through metaphor.

Metaphor has long been used as an extremely effective tool for presenting complex concepts succinctly, and hence more memorably. According to philosopher George Lakoff: "The essence of metaphor is understanding and experiencing one kind of thing in terms of another."

Whenever you can take a set of concepts, processes, or relationships, and place them in a simpler or more familiar setting, you allow your learners' brains to grasp them almost wholesale. This is why I've used the metaphor of the "Sieve" in this book.

You can find good metaphors for your own topics easily. Here's how:

Presentation Technique: Create a Metaphor

Possible metaphors are all around you. Search among things like:

❖ Popular movies, plays, TV shows, or books (notice the plethora of books using metaphor titles, like *The Tao of Pooh, Leadership Secrets of Attila the Hun, Moses on Management,* and—my all-time favorite—*Jesus, CEO!*)

❖ *Genres*—fairy tales, game shows, sports, westerns, science fiction (remember President Reagan and his beloved military program "Star Wars"?), etc.

❖ Major events and holidays (Aren't salespeople always "courting" customers? Possibly every day should be Valentine's Day for your sales trainees.)

❖ Industry settings like courtrooms, factories, farming, mining, deep sea exploration, etc. (Notice how this book keeps referring to the show business industry. After all, isn't every professional communicator something of a performer?)

Not every topic can be easily fitted into an apt metaphor. If after a reasonable effort you can't come up with one for yours, don't despair— as noted above, you have another invaluable meaning-making tool at your disposal:

DOWNTIME

In Chapter 2, you read about the **cycles** and **rhythms** of the brain, which decree when we're in a paying attention mode and when we're in a reflective, or making meaning mode. Specifically, we can receive new information only about 25 percent of the time. The other 75 percent of our time is spent placing it into context. It is only by doing this that our brains can transfer much of it from short-term to long-term memory. If they are not allowed the opportunity, they will let go of it faster than a cat with a stink-beetle. (And take it from a country girl, that's fast.)

What does this mean to teachers and trainers? *First and foremost, that downtime MUST be built into every module.* If your program is too information-dense, you must loosen it up! Separate the Need-to-Know from the Nice-to-Know, and get rid of the latter so as to have time for discussion, Q&A, reflection and writing, frequent review, and many other activities described in this book. For the moment, here is yet another light-touch downtime activity:

> **❝The association and consolidation process can only occur during down time.**
> Dr. Alan Hobson, professor, Harvard University

Learner Activity: Goal Assessment Charts

See Chap 6

Goal Assessment Charts are a great way to ensure focused **peer feedback**. Note that the Goal Assessment Chart is similar to the Pulse-Taking Flip Chart in Chapter 7, but differs slightly in its effects. The flip chart allows

See
Chap 5

your learners to have a say in their own learning at the beginning of the learning module, giving them a sense of **choice** in the overall experience. The Goal Assessment Chart is used by your learners continually throughout, and as such is an admirable tool for providing downtime.

Goal Assessment Charts also provide a great assessment tool for you. Despite the fact that their charts are displayed for all to see, I predict your learners will be amazingly candid in publicly appraising the quality of their work. True, with your encouragement they will use their natural playfulness in devising these charts; but be assured that they will also use this opportunity to discuss their personal and professional goals among themselves, and will list these with great care on their charts. (Just more evidence that you don't have to be solemn to be serious!)

TIME NEEDED

Fifteen minutes and ten seconds

MATERIALS NEEDED

❖ A sheet of flip chart paper for each team

❖ Colored markers

WHAT TO DO

1. Give your class the course goals, and have each team list these, as well any personal goals they might share in taking this course. Encourage them to add one or two eccentric ones. Examples of these might be:

   ❖ "Discover a cure for the common cold."

   ❖ "Come up with three questions that stump the teacher."

   ❖ "Make the other teams wish they were us."

2. Have the teams post their charts on the walls for the duration of the module. Invite all teams to wander around at breaks and read each other's charts.

3. Just before breaks, have team members consult with each other to gauge their own progress on their chart. Encourage them to do their team cheer every time they have made good progress toward a goal. (*Note:* The room will ring with cheers during this time. This is a very good thing! The celebratory sounds will create a positive atmosphere, enhancing brain function; meanwhile each team, hearing cheers all around it, will want to have even more cheers to offer at the next break. It's a **role-model motivation** issue....)

See
Chap 2

TIP
Optional: Tell your learners at the outset that the team goal getting the most laughs from the class will win a Fabulous Prize.

The appendix of this book, "Anatomy of a Creative Learning Module" contains many examples of downtime in a one-day module. For now, let's look at the second way in which you can "use time to save time."

Axe-Sharpener #2: Heightening Attention

Besides needing time to make meaning, the brain seems to need to pause periodically to rebuild attention. You may remember reading in Chapter 2 about Bluma Zeigarnick, the German researcher who found that interrupting a task periodically leads to better recall. Zeigarnick actually considered it optimal to insert a five-minute break every half hour. I myself tend toward two or three minute breaks every forty-five minutes. However you prefer to do it, what kinds of breaks work best? Here are a few options to choose from. I call them "Energizers."

"When I play, it gets me smart for my homework."
Six-year-old

Learner Activity: Two Minutes of Heaven

This activity inspires laughter, Ooh's and Aah's, and a general sense of well-being. It works beautifully with groups that you know are comfortable with physicality. Some people aren't for a variety of personal reasons, while certain cultures and religious groups actually have mandates against cross-gender touching. For these reasons, some organizations prohibit such touching, and you would be wise to check your own company's policy manual just in case. *Key Point:* If you're not absolutely sure about this Energizer, *don't use it!* There are others that will work just as well.

TIME
About two minutes

WHAT TO DO
1. Everyone stands up, stretches, and turns to the right.

2. They now give a one-minute shoulder rub to the person in front of them.

3. They then turn to the left and do it again.

4. They then sit down. That's it.

TIPS
❖ If you want to add an extra dimension—and you have a small group, a spacious room, or "boardroom" style seating—let your learners do this activity standing in a circle. This is fairer anyway, since then there are no end-of-the-row folks who only get one back rub to everyone else's two.

❖ Another idea: After their shoulder rubs, have the entire circle place their hands on each other's shoulders and sit down simultaneously—on each other's laps. (Note: This feat can be accomplished, but gets big laughs one way or the other.)

Learner Activity: Cross Laterals

The brain works best when both halves are equally engaged. But throughout the day, blood flow fluctuates from one side of the brain to the other, making each side alternately dominant. Since the right side of the brain controls the left side of the body and vice versa, "Cross Laterals"—physical movements that engage both sides of the body independently—force the brain to use both hemispheres at once, effectively "talking to itself." This seems to have the effect of equalizing the blood flow to each side, further heightening attention. For this reason, Cross Laterals are particularly good for breaks preceding "Key Point" moments in your programs.

TIME
About two minutes

WHAT TO DO
Lead your learners in two or three of the following activities:

❖ Simultaneously rubbing your stomach and patting your head. Do it one way, then switch hands. (Even those who are good at this have a "preferred mode.")

❖ Touching right hands to left knees (or, behind the body, to left heels); touching opposite elbows and hips; or giving yourself a pat on the back on the opposite side.

❖ Simultaneously swinging one arm forward and the other backward.

❖ Touching your nose with your right hand and your right ear with your left, then switching. Repeat three times.

❖ Holding your finger in front of you at arm's length, move it to the right while you turn your head to the left. Keep your eyes on the finger! Reverse. Do it a few times. Stop before you go blind.

❖ My personal favorite: On a flip chart or overhead, quickly draw a row of arrows, pointing up, down, left, and right. As you draw, have your attendees call out which directions the arrows are pointing. Then draw another row, this time having attendees *turn their heads* in the appropriate directions. Do it a third time, having attendees say in which directions the arrows point, but turn their heads in the *opposite* directions. Do it a fourth time, having them turn their heads in the right directions but say the opposite. Finish by begging them to let you stop before they kill you.

Learner Activity: Scarf Juggling

Juggling with scarves is far easier than with balls, since the scarves move much more slowly through the air. There are many juggling supply stores online, although not all of them sell scarves. For one that does (at good prices), see the endnotes to this chapter.[2]

TIME

Two to five minutes

MATERIALS

You'll need three juggling scarves for each participant.

PREPARATION

You'll want to develop this skill yourself before leading the group. (Don't worry, it won't take long.)

WHAT TO DO

1. Hold the scarves by their corners, two in your left hand, and one in your right. Note: Your hands should be *palm-down*, the scarves dangling from your fingertips.

2. Using a "pulling" motion (that is, keeping the backs of your hands facing upward), toss one of the left-hand scarves up and to the right.

3. Toss the right-hand scarf up and to the left. Catch the first scarf in your right hand as it descends.

4. Toss the second left-hand scarf up and to the right, catching the right-hand scarf on the way down.

5. Keep going. You'll be amazed at how quickly this becomes easy. Just remember: Keep your hands *palm-down.*

Learner Activity: Balloon Breaks

These are fabulous! Balloons are hard to control, yet they don't hurt anyone or damage anything. Plus, of course, they're cheap.

TIME

About two minutes

MATERIALS

Enough balloons to give one to each team

WHAT TO DO

1. Form your learners into *ad hoc* teams of equal numbers. (If any team is short one, join that team yourself.) Have each team stand in a line. Give each team a balloon.

2. Demo how each team must "float" a balloon (that is, tap it but not hand it) down the line and back again. Tell them that if the balloon touches the floor, they must start over. The team that is first to get the balloon to the end of the line and back wins.

3. Call, "Ready, set, go!" and let the games begin.

4. Have everyone kowtow to the winning team, and ask them all to sit back down and get to work.

TIP

There are endless variations to this game: Team members may "float" their balloon using only their elbows, only their heads, "anything but hands," etc. Just remind them to be careful—no diving over chairs to retrieve runaway balloons! (Note: Any team that gets really creative in passing their balloon should receive special recognition from you.)

BIG OLD TIP

It should be acknowledged that "TJ"-type learners[3]—executives, analysts, accountants, programmers, and so on—tend not only to resist half-hour breaks, but to rebel outright against balloons! Yet even they benefit from this brain-based technique. I have found it works best to soberly explain

See
Chap 2
the **Primacy and Recency Effects**. (For really hard cases, use the term "**Zeigarnick Effect**"; TJs tend to respect things that sound foreign.) Uncolored balloons may further soothe their dignity. And when they do find themselves laughing as they play with their balloons, by all means reassure them that they are merely oxygenating their blood.

Reflection Section

How could you show the Big Picture to your learners? Is there a metaphor that would represent your topic well? Where are some specific places in one of your current modules you could insert downtime? Which of the above break activities do you prefer? Do you know of any other safe, appropriate physical activities you could use for your Zeigarnick Breaks? Where do you want to insert them in your existing and planned programs?

....

....

....

....

....

....

....

....

You've now looked at the second way to give the brain time to sharpen its axe. Let's look at the third.

Axe-Sharpener #3: Reviewing Information

When I was nine, my father followed his lifelong dream to own and operate a cattle ranch, and my family subsequently moved from the San Francisco suburbs to a rural valley in the Canadian Cascade Mountains. This, almost certainly, is another story for another day—the part that's relevant here is this. . .

As one of thousands of city girls who were crazy for horses, I couldn't keep away from ours. Besides riding them constantly, I popped up beside them in pastures, corrals, and stalls. Since I usually had food or a currycomb in my hands, the horses seemed to have no problem with my visits. Nonetheless, my father kept telling me not to come up on them from behind, lest I startle them and get kicked. He took to intoning it like a chant: "Never sneak up behind a horse and take it by surprise." *"Never sneak up behind a horse and take it by surprise."* "NEVER SNEAK UP BEHIND A HORSE AND TAKE IT BY SURPRISE."

Finally one day, just as I was about to slip up behind one of our horses munching hay in its stall, I got an unexpected hit of wariness: *Was I taking the animal by surprise?*

I made a deliberate noise. The horse looked around with a slightly bored expression (something they adopt for most occasions, as it turns out), and I entered without incident to perform my usual abeyances. To this day—unlike some others who have hung around horses as much as I—I have yet to be kicked by a horse. The frequent review my father had provided made my brain decide the information was important.

Why does your brain believe that remembering repeated information will *keep you alive?* Well, think about it: What if every day you had to relearn how to deal with the many things that happen to you regularly, like tying your shoes or driving a car? You would be baby-like, nearly helpless. Maybe your brain figures that if you've encountered information numerous times in the past, you might reasonably expect to encounter it again. Better pay attention to it!

In Chapter 2, you read about the findings of Hermann Ebbinghaus regarding the typical "Curve of Forgetting," and the positive effects of regular **review** on learner recall. The fact is that any program can and should be designed to include regular periods of review. Here are some easy ways to build these into your programs.

Presentation Technique: Group Chants

(Note: Use this in an ad hoc way throughout your module.)

Colin Rose says repetition without *personal involvement* is ineffectual. Simple drilling on previously learned material can allow misunderstandings to go undetected. It can also be boring, which is of course highly brain-antagonistic. Used sparingly, group chants offer a fun, flexible, slightly quirky way of reviewing main points.

PREPARATION

Start by deciding what are the primary and secondary concepts in your curriculum. Any principle that shows up in all skills would be a Primary concept, while any principle that shows up frequently will be a Secondary concept. For example, in planning a program on Professional Telephone Skills, the common elements in all the skills being taught might be *Competence* and *Caring*. (I've found that each attribute is necessary, but neither is sufficient without the other. Ever leave an urgent message with a receptionist who seems competent, but doesn't seem to care, or one who seems to care, but doesn't appear competent? Both instances are worrisome, aren't they?) I then find some secondary, more specific categories, like *Sharing the Power*, and *Keeping It Positive*.

WHAT TO DO

Keep relating back to the Primary and Secondary concepts by having your learners finish your sentences for you. For example, throughout the Telephone Skills program, I say things like: "Giving callers the extension number before transferring them allows you to. . . ." "Share the Power," the class responds. "Which makes them feel that you. . . ." "Care," they intone.

"Thanking customers for holding instead of apologizing allows you to. . . ." "Keep it Positive," my learners say. "Which makes them feel that you are. . . ." "Competent," they chant. You get the idea.

This repetition technique offers an opportunity for playful involvement, and also continually puts information into context. Both things are great **intrinsic motivators** for the brain.

See Chap 2

TIP

Your attendees might see this technique as a mindless practice reminiscent of cults. And it is true that if you overuse it, it will quickly become annoying. Still, the tactic can be highly effective as an impromptu review technique. Meanwhile, let's remember that initial reticence on the part of learners is never a reason to reject any activity out of hand. (If it were, no trainer would ever get to do role-plays, and you know how valuable those can be!) The secret to using this technique effectively lies in *managing learner perceptions* about the activity. You do this through trust and humor. If you haven't built their trust, learners won't take part in this or many other training activities. Here's how to use a little humor to give this activity extra appeal:

1. Wait in silence for your learners to finish your sentence. Then, when they don't (and they seldom do at first), look sincerely quizzical as if to say, "What? I thought you folks *knew* this one." You will feel the energy begin to heighten as they wonder what the heck you want from them.

2. If they still don't speak, lean forward, put a hand to your ear, and adopt a hopeful expression. Finally they will get it, take pity on you, and come across. Your tenaciousness—and self-deprecation—will have tickled and disarmed them.

After a while, your learners will come to expect this little ritual—and even instinctively get what it's all about. Their chants will become quick and enthusiastic throughout the program. (As long as it's not overused!)

Learner Activity: Study-Buddy Teaching

(Note: Use this every ten to fifteen minutes throught your module.)

TIME

About two minutes.

PREPARATION

At the beginning of any learning module, have your learners form "Study Buddy" duos with the people sitting next to them. Ask the duos to look at each other and decide who has the bigger head. That will be Buddy A; the other person will be Buddy B. They will remain so throughout the module.

MATERIALS

An egg-timer might be helpful to keep you on track.

WHAT TO DO

1. At about the ten-minute mark, stop your lecture and ask your "A" Buddies to pretend that their "B" Buddies just walked into the room, missing everything that was said in the last ten minutes. Give them one minute to explain the main points.

2. Take any questions your learners might have. (Note: If there are questions that will be answered later in the program, congratulate the questioner on their foresight, and ask them to "hold onto that thought.")

3. At the next ten-minute mark, switch off: Have the "B" Buddies explain the curriculum to the "A's."

4. Keep doing this throughout the module.

Learner Activity: Finish-the-Sentence Ball Toss

(Note: Use this when you want to conduct your one-day review at the *end of the module.*)

This great review technique was practiced at the Lozanov Learning

Institute in Washington. It allowed teachers to assess not only the conscious but also the **non-conscious learning** of their students.

See Chap 2

TIME
About ten minutes

WHAT TO DO

1. Ask a curriculum question to a learner, simultaneously throwing a ball to them.

2. The learner answers with whatever comes to them as they catch the ball.

3. That's it.

In this seemingly simple-minded game, you are *deliberately distracting your learners from conscious thought* by focusing them on an immediate physical action. This allows the knowledge that is stored in one of the **implicit pathways** to surface and become **explicit**. Time and again at the Lozanov Institute, students were heard to say, "I was surprised I knew the answer. It just popped up!"

See Chap 2

A TIP
This game can be modified to have learners ask each other questions as they toss the ball, allowing for more **peer feedback**. In this case, your job is to interject questions on any key points they may miss.

See Chap 6

ANOTHER TIP
Be sure to use this as an assessment tool! If no one asks a question about a key point, it may be that they didn't think about it; if no one knows the answer when you ask it, it is definitely because you somehow failed to convey it well enough. Good to know!

Learner Activity: Today's Experts

(Note: Use this when you want to conduct your one-day review at the *beginning of the next day's module*.)

As well as reinforcing information by allowing your learners to think creatively about it, this activity will give them that all-important "You Are Here" context into which they can fit the new information you're about to deliver.

TIME

Fifteen to twenty minutes

PREPARATION

At the end of each daily module, assign one to three learners to summarize that day's material at the beginning of the next day. Tell them that they will have five to ten minutes to present their summaries, either through **mind maps** or demonstration.

See Chap 7

WHAT TO DO

1. At the beginning of each module, welcome your learners back, and then lead applause for "Today's Experts."

2. Give your Experts their allotted time to recap the material of the previous day.

3. Take questions from the audience. Allow your Experts first crack at answering these. If they answer correctly, lead admiring applause. If they give inaccurate answers, take the error onto yourself: Acknowledge that what you said must have *sounded* this way (let's face it, it did to your Experts), and then clarify what you really meant to convey. This tactic will allow your learners to feel free to ask questions throughout all your modules.

4. One last time, lead applause for "Today's Experts," and invite them to take their seats bathed in glory.

Learner Activity: Dr. Truth

(Note: This game works well for review of a week's worth of material.)
Three learners will start the following week with a recap of the previous

week's main points. The catch: They will include some incorrect information in their presentations. The other learners will try to identify which parts of the presentations are accurate and which are not.

PREPARATION

At the end of the week, assign a three-person group to prepare a presentation about the main points of the week's curriculum. (Note: You might want to give them a list of the main points.) Then start the first module of the next week with "Dr. Truth."

MATERIALS

You'll need a picture of a pair of trousers with flames coming off them. (Note: Your own drawing on an 8½ x 11 sheet of paper will be more than sufficient.) This will be the winner's award.

TIME

Twenty to thirty minutes

WHAT TO DO

1. At the beginning of class, invite the three-person review group up to the front of the class, and have one member begin reviewing the first point. The listeners should be on the lookout for inaccuracies and misinformation, and jot down any they hear.

2. After the first speaker finishes, the listeners get to raise their hands and point out which facts were wrong. Each erroneous fact that the audience does *not* catch counts as a point for the speaker, as does each correct fact that is identified as incorrect.

3. Repeat this process with the other two speakers.

4. The presenter who got the most points—slipped the most fibs past their fellow learners—wins. Award them the coveted "Liar, Liar, Pants on Fire" award, and invite all the players to take their seats amid applause.

See
Chap 2

TIP

Advise your presenters that they will do best at this game if they keep their fibs subtle. Remember, they want to stump their fellow learners, while *you* want to make everyone think hard about the material. On the other hand, a little "over the top" stuff will add liveliness to the game, so by all means remind them that they will get bonus points for laughs!

Learner Activity: Game Show

(Note: This is a great wrap-up review of an entire program.)

WHAT TO DO

Use the formats of popular TV shows, like "Jeopardy," for example. Plenty of software exists to present your review material in game show format. In particular, The Trainer's Warehouse[4] offers a good selection. If you don't have the budget for software, you can still create blackboard, whiteboard, or flip-chart replications of these shows' Question Boards. If you have neither budget, time, nor materials, just write the questions on index cards for your own use. However you handle your logistics, all you really have to do for this activity is divide your learners into two groups, and go for it!

TIPS

❖ Offering prizes will add to the fun of this game (assuming they aren't extrinsically motivating; for more on intrinsically motivating prizes, see Chapter 5).

❖ Copyright-free "game show" music can also be had cheaply through The Trainer's Warehouse.

Learner Activity: Music and Poetry Corner

(Note: This one is equally appropriate at the end of a day, a module, or the entire program.)

Have your teams make up poems, rap, or pop songs about salient segments of the learning material. Besides the **rhyme**, **rhythm**, and **music** boosting brain function, this is great for providing **peer feedback**, not to mention ending the segment on a **celebratory** note.

See
Chap 6
&
Chap 2

TIME NEEDED

About 45 minutes

WHAT TO DO

1. Tell your teams you want them to write and perform a song, rap, or poem that includes the main points of that day's curriculum. Inform them they will get five points for each key fact included and three points for each secondary fact (as well as the usual bonus points for laughs and creativity). Ask them to choose a team spokesperson, and tell them they have twenty-three and three-quarter minutes to prepare their performance.

2. At the end of twenty-three and three-quarter minutes, call time, and have each team perform for the class.

3. After each performance, have the spokesperson reinforce learning by enumerating each concept their piece dealt with. Then let the entire team take questions.

4. Give points accordingly throughout, tell the teams their scores, and have them take their seats to thunderous applause.

Before we leave this topic, a final note: Besides anchoring information, review allows learners to achieve a very important **state** called "Knowing They Know." Ever had a learner who you darned well *knew* understood the curriculum, but who didn't believe it himself? It was as good as his not knowing it at all, right? He felt uncertain, unwilling to go forward. Review is a useful tool for helping learners to know they've got the material. For this and the other reasons noted above, frequent review is imperative in all your modules. You should use it religiously.

See
Chap 2

> **"People's beliefs about their abilities have a profound effect on those abilities."**
> Albert Bandura, Stanford University psychologist

Reflection Section

How can you get yourself into the habit of including frequent review, if you aren't already? Insert reminders as you design your curriculum? Use an egg timer or stopwatch? Use Break Managers (Chapter 5)? Are you clear on the Primary and Secondary points in your programs? Besides the techniques described in this chapter, can you think of other ways you might build more review into your programs?

....

....

....

....

....

....

....

....

....

....

Some Next Steps

1. See if you can come up with a solid metaphor for your topic.

2. Buy some juggling scarves and begin practicing.

3. Get some balloons and *use them!*

4. Look over your existing programs: Keeping the "Need-to-Know" material, can you cut out some "Nice-to-Know" stuff and replace it with review?

5. Look over your existing programs: What are the Primary and Secondary concepts? Use these in Group Chants.

6. List some ways to break Study Buddy duos into Partners A and B. Examples: Partners A are the ones with the shortest nails, or the coolest pen, or the most coins in their pocket, or. . . .

7. Get a small, *SOFT* ball for Finish-the-Sentence Ball Toss.

8. Make (or ask your students or maybe your children to make) a Jeopardy board. Write review questions on 3 x 5 cards. Watch Alex Trebec, the host of "Jeopardy"; buy a false mustache; *be* Alex Trebec! (Okay, this last part is optional, but if you do it, be sure to include a couple of questions about Canada, Trebec's homeland. Remember to look reproachful, as he always does, when your American audience doesn't know the answers.)

You have now looked at a number of ways to insert "breathers" into your programs. Remember: Good learning takes time, yet in the end breathers are the best time management strategy you can practice. In addition, I herewith promise again that you don't need to cut your curriculum by much in order to employ breathers.

Once more I am reminded of the one-day Traffic Violator classes I used to teach. These were not only sanctioned by the people at the California Department of Motor Vehicles, but also designed by them. Whether those folks were credentialed curriculum designers I know not—but talk about dense curriculum! On first glance, it seemed impossible that one could deliver it in any other way than through rapid-fire lecture. Yet my highly creative comedians and I found ways to impart the whole of that information (as we were mandated to do by *state law*, thank you very much) in a rollicking, interactive one-day session. People regularly left our classes saying things like, "I didn't think I needed this, but I did. Thank you." This would never have happened if they had sat through a whole day of lecture! Creative Learning can always be used, if you care enough.

Whew! At this point you now know: 1) what humor is, 2) why you should use it, and 3) many ways in which you can use it successfully. You have, if I may say so, a bulging toolbox of tips, tricks, games, and techniques that will help make learning the engrossing experience it should be. More importantly, you have an understanding of the principles that will support you in your decision to use these strategies in your own work.

But wait—it's not Grad Night yet. We still have a couple of matters to address, and the first one has to do with the questions I most often receive about Creative Learning. These questions are many and varied, but essentially they all express one main concern:

MAIN CONCERN

What if, in spite of all my practice in Creative Learning,
my use of humor somehow goes
terribly,
h o r r i b l y
W R O N G ?

If you have any lingering fears along those lines (and you quite legiti-mately may, in spite of my shameless attempts throughout this book to manage your **state** into one of boundless enthusiasm), then I have this to say to you...

See
Chap 2

PART III
THE "WHO, ME?"

laugh in the
face of fear!

THE ROOKIE police officer shot down the freeway in his shiny
new prowler. The V-8 engine hummed power, the lights flashed,
the siren issued a satisfying blare of city-sanctioned authority.

It was the rookie's first official call of duty: a traffic collision.
And he was ready, more than ready. All his life he had dreamed

only of one thing—being a cop. He'd studied hard at the Police Academy, he'd graduated at the top of his class. Now he was going to bring law enforcement to a whole new level. . . .

Rounding a curve, he could see the accident up ahead. Looked like a bad one, he thought grimly. It also looked as if he was the first officer on the scene. Pulling to the side, he emerged from his car—and was met by the most grisly sight he had ever beheld: an arm lying in the ditch.

As if by a wizard's stroke, everything he had learned at the Police Academy disappeared. In a panic he struggled to recall his training, but to no avail; his mind was as free of information as a newborn babe's. This was terrible, he thought wildly. His first career challenge, and he was going to fail! It couldn't be!

With a huge force of will, the rookie shut his eyes and called up before him a comforting image of the Police Procedures Manual. It worked—in his mind's eye, he could clearly see the title, "Chapter 8: Traffic Accidents," and right after that, "Section 1: Unattended Body Parts."

Of course! He knew what to do when there was an arm lying in a ditch: You write a report.

Hastily drawing forth his pristine, new report pad and sharp, new pencil, he carefully wrote:

"A-R-M in D-I-T-C-H."

Back in the saddle now, he began to stride confidently around the scene. He saw a leg in the ditch. He flipped to a new page.

"L-E-G," he wrote, "in D-I-T-C-H."

Humming a little tune, he continued walking about. Suddenly he came upon a human head lying right in the middle of the boulevard. He had a moment of renewed shock. Quickly he pulled himself back together.

"H-E-A-D," he wrote, "in. . ."

He stopped. He looked around. Then, giving an oh-so-gentle kick, he finished:

"D-I-T-C-H."

❖   ❖   ❖

In the foregoing (as in so many jokes), we learn an important truth: The most courageous among us will sometimes avoid doing things—even little things—if we don't think we'll do them well. You, for instance, may deeply believe in the value of humor as a communication and teaching device, but feel it's something you personally shouldn't attempt. Specifically, you may believe one of four things:

> **"A person becomes brave by doing brave things."**
> Plato, philosopher

1. My audience or subject is too serious for humor.

2. I'm not funny!

3. I might offend someone.

4. I won't be able to control laughing learners.

If you hold to any of these beliefs, then I have very good news for you: They're all myths. Let's take the easiest one first.

Fear #1: "My Audience/Subject Is Too Serious"

The short answer is, you could be right, but with respect I doubt it. Witness this excerpt from *PS* (August 1993), the U.S. army's magazine of preventive maintenance:

> A slipping gear could let your M203 grenade launcher fire when you least expect it. That would make you quite unpopular in what's left of your unit.

I have yet to see an audience that is too serious for a little appropriate humor. Even the most task-oriented, "TJ" learners use humor—just ask an engineer about the mnemonic for memorizing color sequences on resistors. (Unfortunately it can't be reprinted here, being in purely awful taste.) The fact is that, given a choice between having some fun and not having any, everybody prefers having some fun. Everybody.

As for serious subjects: John Cleese of Monty Python fame once said, "You don't have to be solemn to be serious." And he should know. Since

1972, through Video Arts, he has provided corporations worldwide with funny training videos on a range of vital business topics. Cleese makes the excellent point that we actually laugh most about those things most serious to us, like money ("Inflation is what lets you live in a more expensive house without having to move"); sex ("If it's such a private thing, why do we have to do it with another person?"); our children ("If Abraham's son had been a teenager, it wouldn't have been a sacrifice!"); even death (Oscar Wilde's actual last words: "Either this wallpaper goes, or I do."). The bottom line is that no matter how serious your topic, your listeners need to relax about and open up to it. Humor can allow them to do this quickly—as long as it is used appropriately, another subject we will examine in depth in this chapter.

> **❝To be playful and serious at the same time is possible, and it defines the ideal mental condition.❞**
> John Dewey, nineteenth-century philosopher and educational theorist

Fear #2: "I'm Not Funny!"

I can hear you now: "I'm not! I don't get half the jokes people tell *me*. I forget punchlines. People look at me and *they* forget punchlines. I am the Terminator of Humor."

Well, as luck would have it, the answer is simple: *Don't try to be "funny"—just try to have fun.* This is the one rule about humor that most amateur comedians get wrong. Too often they're playing "Look at Me, I'm the Next Robin Williams," and they come across as egotistical. And no matter what some comedy fans may think, the point of humor is not about fame, but fun. You don't have to be Robin Williams if you're having a good time.

A good place to start is to ask yourself why you want to use humor at all. (I'm assuming you do if you're reading this book.) Most people want to for one of two reasons:

1. To receive approval and/or attention

2. To connect more enjoyably with their fellow human beings

People who use humor mostly to get *approval* tend not to care about their listeners. Their humor is ego-focused: They stop us in the hall when we're in a hurry, and tell us the latest Internet joke; they disrupt meetings with a quip they just can't keep to themselves; they derail productive conversations with, "That reminds me of the one. . . ." All just to hijack a few moments of our already-overtaxed attention. People who use humor primarily to *connect,* on the other hand, simply see delightful things about the world in general—including us, their conversation partners! They appreciate anything that inspires laughter; it doesn't have to come from them. Essentially, they use humor to keep from taking themselves too seriously (another ego-focused act), and to lighten things up in general. Their main contribution is not that they are always ready with a joke, but that they are often ready with a laugh.

To summarize: You don't have to be screamingly funny to be seen as someone with a "great sense of humor." You just have to be naturally fun. Fortunately for you, this is easy—as you admitted in Chapter 4, you're a former child, which means you *are* naturally fun! We've all seen the person who tells a so-so joke, but laughs so hard telling it that we just have to laugh along. Ask yourself: Whom do you prefer to see coming down the hall, the Spotlight-Grabber or the Fun-Lover? So be the Fun-Lover.

And now for. . .

Fear #3 (and the Only Well-Founded Fear): "Will I Offend Someone?"

The rule here is amazingly simple: *To avoid inappropriate humor, simply avoid derogatory humor.*

Think about this one. As a child, you were undoubtedly taught not to say things like, "Hey stupid," "Hey fatty," or "Hey ugly!" Yet how many adults today use put-down humor as their main staple? True, these put-downs might be a bit more sophisticated than "Hey, stupid." Maybe these hilarious adults prefer jibes like, "He's so dense light bends *around* him," or "When you stand next to her, you can hear the ocean," or "That guy is depriving a village somewhere of an idiot." Okay, arguably funny. And okay, comics like Don Rickles have made a good living by using such material almost exclusively. But as I'm sure you realize, what's appropriate in comedy clubs often—in fact, usually—isn't appropriate in the real world.

And now for a quick story: I have a friend who is so funny that I have literally heard people beg her to stop talking so they could simply inhale. As it happens, this woman has a positive gift for the elegantly worded insult. Just to give you an idea, once when I was becoming quite animated about something or other, she told me I "looked like a Chihuahua on speed." I of course laughed on this occasion, just as I did every time she made such comments. But after a number of such jokes, I one day drew her aside and privately asked whether there was anything wrong between us.

"No," she answered in sincere surprise. "I tease everyone that way. Haven't you noticed?"

Of course I had. Still, I pursued the matter a bit further just to be sure. Then, once satisfied that our friendship was on solid ground (and after getting her to promise that if she ever really was angry at me she'd tell me so), I let the subject drop.

Okay, first remember that this woman is a close friend of mine. And now let me put a question to you: If *you* use derogatory humor with someone who is not a close friend—say, someone at a meeting, or one of your learners—what are the chances *they* will request a private audience to work on your relationship? I think you know the answer: Pretty slim. Instead they will almost certainly remember your sarcasm for months if not years to come, will always suspect that you harbor some hostility toward them—*and will never ask.* Your relationship will always be a bit strained, and you will always wonder why. Isn't this too high a price to pay for getting a laugh?

Understand something further: This is not just an issue of interpersonal relations. If you refuse to put anyone down, by logical extension you can't inadvertently put down any subgroup in our society—minorities, women, seniors, Gen-Xers, or anyone else. In other words, *avoid derogatory humor and you need NEVER worry about using humor inappropriately again!*

Didn't I tell you it was simple?

Okay, actually, you are allowed to use sarcastic humor against one person, and one person only. Can you guess who that is? Right: yourself! In Chapter 6 you saw how self-deprecating humor can work wonders in reducing distance between people. This means that I, for example, may freely make jokes deriding redheads or Baby-Boomers, because I quite obviously am one. I may also make jokes about Americans, native Californians, or people of Scandinavian descent for the same reason—although since it's not necessarily obvious that I am one of these, I would be wise to preface the jokes with, "I'm an American/native Californian/Danish, so I can tell this joke." Under no circumstances, however, may I make cracks about senior citizens or men, since (obviously, I hope) I'm not one.

> **"When managers tell [bigoted] jokes, whether or not anyone of the affected class is present, they parcel up their careers and hand them out to everyone listening."**
>
> Al Pozos, manager, Pacific Bell

Make sense? Good, because now we get to the only ever-so-slightly tricky part of the whole business: Although I may not make Jewish jokes since I am not Jewish, *even my Jewish friends may run into trouble if they do*. Why? Because that particular brand of humor is controversial. Anytime you're dealing with controversy, you are on shaky ground.

In general, the four subjects generally perceived as controversial are:

1. Race or ethnicity.

2. Religion.

3. Obscenity—that is, anything with sexual or scatological content. (I myself howl at scatological jokes, but I try to tell them only to people whom I know to be as juvenile as I am. I never use them in a professional setting.)

4. Partisan politics. Political references can be okay, but beware of being perceived as leaning toward one party or another, or attendees will inevitably complain in their evaluations that you "made political statements all day." If you make a lighthearted comment that seems to denigrate (or praise) one party, you need to follow it up by doing the same to the opposing side. At the very least, you must offer a mitigating quip along with the negative comment. Comedian Jack Mayberry demonstrated this beautifully when he said, "I voted for the Democrats because I didn't like the way the Republicans were running the country. Which is turning out to be like shooting yourself in the head to stop your headache."

In speaking for purposes other than entertainment, here is my personal rule of thumb for avoiding inappropriateness: *If the remark you're contemplating will not offend anyone from the N.O.W., the N.R.A., the Gay/Lesbian Alliance, or the Moral Majority, you get an A!* Otherwise, there are plenty of innocuous subjects—"So I buy this used car"—to have fun with. Stick to those.

And finally, your trainees now aflame with the joy of learning, comes the moment you might well experience the final fear:

Fear #4: "How Do I *Control* These People?"

I will not pretend here that Creative Learning is as tidy as the other kind. I will only remind you that its benefits far outweigh its challenges. Think of Mother Nature in her wild state: unkempt forests, weird-looking deep-water fish, volcanoes, earthquakes. Yes, our Mom seems chaotic. Yet no one will deny that beneath her chaos is an underlying order. I hope I have convinced you by now that the truly humorous, truly creative person is at home with a certain amount of irregularity, confident that underneath the surface important work is going on. Neither creativity nor humor can flourish where perfectionistic rigidity is the rule.

Having said that, here are some tried-and-true techniques for two important aspects of crowd control: keeping attention throughout your program, and bringing groups back to order after breaks, activities, and the like. Let's take the first one first.

KEEPING ATTENTION

Let's start with the good news: As Southwest Airlines has found with their flight safety presentations, when you use humor, you are already ahead of the game—people will pay more attention. However, at those times when your listeners are also using humor, you will have to work a bit harder to maintain your Alpha position, so to speak. Fortunately, this also is pretty easy. Here are three techniques to help you do so.

> **"A leader without a sense of humor is apt to be like the grass mower at the cemetery—he has lots of people under him, but nobody is paying him much attention."**
>
> **Bob Ross,**
> **"The Corporate Comic"**

Presentation Technique: Voice Inflection

(Note: Not to be confused with yelling.) Use lots of vocal variety. Hurry the pace, then slow it down for key information; speak in varying degrees of volume. To perfect this skill fast, tape record yourself over several lectures and listen back. Your weak points will jump out at you.

Presentation Technique: Expressive Body Movement

Find ways to use more than just your hands; again, become something of a performer. A good trick is to imagine that your students don't speak English; this will help you to express yourself through facial expression, body posture, and tone of voice. Even better, take an acting class—preferably in theatre improvisation. I am so fanatical about theatre improvisation because, in addition to being a tremendously fun discipline, it simultaneously gives training in authentic expressiveness, as well as creativity, teamwork, and Zen. If every high school included improv training, I firmly believe the world would be a better place.

Presentation Technique: Asking Questions

Questions affect the brain more powerfully than statements. I've found that they're also subtle attention-getters. In your delivery, try to phrase statements as questions as often as possible. For example, instead of: "The biggest challenges in teaching groups of more than thirty people are. . ." try: "What do you think are the biggest challenges in teaching groups of more than thirty people?" Instead of telling your Customer Service trainees the best way to deal with an angry customer, ask: "What do you think is the best way to respond to an abusive customer?" Then let them discuss possible strategies. Keep on asking questions! And try to make some of them funny!

(Note: This is usually not difficult. For instance, instead of asking, "Why should you not tell an angry customer to 'calm down'?" you might ask, "What do people usually say when they hear the words 'Calm down'?" Or better yet, "What do *you* say when you hear those words?" Your canny learners will yell delightedly: "I AM CALM!")

Key Point: Questions keep people thinking, and allow them to better "own" the material.

BRINGING GROUPS TO ORDER

Again, Creative Learning isn't always orderly. Here are two ways to adroitly recapture attention when distractions arise:

Presentation Technique: Unusual Sounds

This is a quickie, and one you will probably use often: At the end of exercises, discussions, and other break-outs, clink two drinking glasses together, ring a traveling alarm clock, toss a pen into the air and get the attendees nearest you to applaud till it falls back into your hand, or use any of the wide variety of noisemakers obtainable at novelty or magic stores. (Note: Trainer's Warehouse also has a nice selection of these.)

Key Point: Unexpected sounds grab attention and momentarily pique interest in you.

And now for the issue I promised to address way back in Chapter 1: How to take creative risks in front of other people without losing face or control of your environment. Yes, folks, that's right, it's time for:

NOODLING AROUND WITHOUT LOOKING LIKE A MEATBALL!

As you now know, creativity sometimes involves slipping up—"bombing," in comedy club terms. In our world, bombing has less to do with telling jokes that fall flat, and more to do with verbal gaffes, PowerPoint glitches, spilling our notes onto the floor, or losing our pants in front of two hundred public seminar attendees. (That last one has been done, I happen to know.) You may also know from experience that whenever the group leader slips up, there is almost always a ripple of disorder among the group. Depending on the group (and the enormity of the slip-up), this ripple can start to feed on itself. In the worst cases—like when there are low levels of trust and respect in the learning environment—it can result in general confusion and discord.

It goes without saying, I hope, that no technique in this book will inspire your listeners' respect unless you've done your homework and offered them a thoughtful, well-designed program. Assuming that you have, you most certainly can make a few public mistakes without losing an ounce of credibility with your learners, or control of your learning environment. Following are some techniques that will help you to do so.

In Chapter 4, you learned about Acknowledging the Bomb. This will always represent the single most effective way to take a few risks in your delivery while maintaining the credibility and goodwill necessary for keeping order. But now here's a further tip: *Any group leader must be prepared to acknowledge her attendees' bombs as well as her own—to step in and save THEM from looking like "meatballs"!*

It is imperative that you develop this ability; it is the final, indispensable skill for making your learners feel safe with their own creativity. Come up with "ad libs" for typical learner gaffes. When a team presentation is starting to go on too long: "This is so good I don't want to stop you. Hey—does anyone mind staying late. . .? What? Why not?" When a learner's joke or gag flops: "You know what was wrong with that joke? It was too intelligent to be funny. You want to watch that." (Remember, your "ad libs" should be positive in nature, never derogatory.)

Here's a game aimed at helping *your learners* get comfortable with bombing. I heartily recommend using this to introduce them to the concept of creativity, and certainly before giving them their first creative exercise. It is best played with groups of up to fifteen. If you have larger numbers, you might want to demonstrate it first with ten or so attendees, then do breakouts.

Learner Activity: Numbers Horseshoe[1]

This game offers a laughter-filled way to understand that "bombing" is okay as long as we are good-natured about it. Try it and see: Failure can be amazingly unthreatening when it is taken lightly by the Failer.

TIME NEEDED
Ten to fifteen minutes

WHAT TO DO

1. The group stands in a horseshoe formation. Count off down the line so that each player has a number.

2. The first person—Number One—calls out someone else's number: "Twelve!" That person *immediately* shouts out someone else's number: "Five!" That person quickly shouts out another number: "Eight!" and so on. The first person to hesitate at all, or call a wrong number (either their own or one that doesn't exist), relinquishes their place and goes to the end of the line. They, and all who were previously behind them in the lineup, now have different numbers. The game resumes.

3. As it continues, people will constantly blow it, and have to move to the end of the line. Here's the thing: Rather than clenching

their fists, grimacing, or yowling, they must throw their arms up in triumph and trot with pride to the "Loser's" place. Everyone else must applaud said "Loser."

DEBRIEF

Ask the group the following questions:

❖ How did it feel to make light of minor failure? How did it feel to watch someone else do it?

❖ Why are we usually inclined to gnash our teeth and groan when we fail—even in (let's face it) a silly little game that has no bearing on our real lives?

❖ *Key Point:* Are there any other minor failures you have made too much of in your life?

A TIP

Keep the pace so fast that everybody (including you) fails a lot! Besides giving learners lots of practice in the "Ta-Da," this also helps get them into a bold, pleasurable "No Fear" state of mind for further training.

Finally, here's one trick that works magically in those instances when an attendee, flushed with the excitement of the moment, blurts out something in truly questionable taste. Yes, this does happen—not often, but sometimes. If it should happen in your class, try a gentle gag that many comedians use with hecklers. (In case you don't know the term, hecklers are audience members who disrupt a comedian's routine with their own "contributions." Sometimes these contributions are funny, although more often they're not.) The gag allows the comedian to maintain the reins of control by *briefly* making the heckler part of the act—essentially giving them the moment of attention they so obviously crave. I call the technique simply, "The Look."

> **"The greatest mistake you can make in life is to be continually fearing you will make one."**
> Elbert Hubbard,
> author and publisher

Presentation Technique: "The Look"

WHAT TO DO

1. Stop speaking. Immediately.

2. Turn your head to look at the speaker. (Note: Turn the *head*, not just the eyes. If the learner in question is directly in front of you, do the "double-take": Look at them, away, then back again.)

3. Look bland (not serious, just bland). This is pure luxury—each onlooker will attribute to you the emotion they consider appropriate; you will offend no one!

4. Hold the look about three seconds. This builds the laugh. Continue holding the look until the laugh begins to subside.

5. Smile slightly, maybe narrow your eyes a bit—I call it the "We Have a Secret, You and I" look—and carry on as before. (Note: Don't be tempted to ignore this step! The recipient will feel you saw some meaning in their remark that was deeper than even they knew. They will feel vaguely validated, and accept your moving on.)

That's it: The Look. It defuses. It says, "It's okay, we all know you meant well; now let's move forward." It turns potentially awkward situations into team-building experiences 99.9 percent of the time. Why? Because the recipient usually *did* mean well! All they wanted was a laugh. And they got it, compliments of you.

And now for a particularly important tip: *Be aware that humorous responses are emphatically NOT appropriate for all awkward situations.* When an attendee is sincerely concerned or upset, a humorous response from you will seem flippant. If someone utters a bigoted remark in your classroom, humor from you will seem worse than flippant. (Indeed, in your leadership position you cannot afford even the appearance of condoning such remarks.) However, as noted above, most learner gaffes are well intended, and require only the lightest touch to steer things back on track. It is here that humor can stand you in excellent stead.

And now for one final, and very important, method of maintaining control:

FIRM, UNWAVERING INSISTENCE!

Let me say it again: Some disorderly behavior is inevitable when learners are inspired and energized. The most common kind by far is what I call "Post Exercise Glow," wherein teams can't quite let go of a practice session to turn their attention back to the classroom at large. A certain amount of Post Exercise Glow is unavoidable (and is a big compliment to your teaching, by the way). The rule is simply not to let it spread like wildfire.

Presentation Technique: Leaning on Them Lightly

WHAT TO DO

❖ Always respond good-naturedly *but immediately* to any sustained buzz when you are holding the floor. Examples:

– "Some question I can answer over there?"

– "So as I was saying—*Bob*—(raise one eyebrow and smile) was. . ."

❖ If these strategies don't work, it's perfectly okay to make a general announcement like: "I want everyone to feel free to make comments. But no one will hear them unless they're addressed to the class at large. Individual conversations just won't cut it."

❖ Reinforce these verbal messages with nonverbal ones: Stop talking until your chronic chatterers stop, or simply move to stand near them as you continue lecturing (this always results in a sudden suspension of conversation).

Key Point: Keep it light, but keep it up!

It may seem paradoxical that crowd control is particularly important in Creative Learning, but such is the case. Look at it like this: If you are a parent, you know that no matter how much they may resist, children feel safer when limits are set for them. We adults are really not so different, especially when we are confronted with the unfamiliar, when we tend to revert to early-learned behaviors. Remember that an environment of spontaneity and risk-taking is probably fairly unfamiliar to most of your learners. They will make mistakes as they rediscover this territory— they will bomb. My experience has shown conclusively that this is never fatal. All that's needed is a willingness on your part to accept and even applaud mistakes as evidence of progress, and to set up a sort of guard rail of control, allowing them to play freely without fear of injury.

> **People who don't take risks generally make about two big mistakes a year. People who do take risks generally make about two big mistakes a year.**
>
> Peter Drucker,
> business philosopher

Reflection Section

Get together with a colleague, or your teaching team as a whole. Discuss the fears you all may have about using humor appropriately and successfully. Do the benefits of humor outweigh the fears? Refer to the solutions laid out in this chapter (giving special attention to the topic of inappropriate humor). After you've explored the issue of fear, play a game from Chapter 4, and see if people then feel more confident in using their natural sense of humor and creativity. If they do, give yourselves a rousing cheer!

I sincerely hope this discussion has eased your concerns about bringing humor into your learning environment. Of course, nothing eliminates anxiety like repeated success. I consider it my great good fortune that I cut my teeth, so to speak, on Traffic Violator School. You just can't get a more unwilling learner than one who is mandated to attend a class because of an infraction. And yet within three months I lost all apprehension of confronting such learners. Why? *Because I had discovered that these techniques worked every single time.* No matter how hostile a learner might be at the beginning of the day, I came to know without doubt that they would be on my side before morning break. And I wasn't even very good at this stuff yet! I made a lot of mistakes—mistakes of which you, in reading this book, are the beneficiary. But people forgave me, because 1) they felt my enthusiasm, 2) they could see I had worked hard on my presentation, and most importantly, 3) I focused outward (always remember, people will cut you a boatload of slack when they get to be "part of the act").

❖   ❖   ❖

I know what you're wondering: Okay, I've got the *what,* the *why,* and the *how.* I'm a gosh-darned Creative Learning whiz. Now is it Grad Night?

And I must answer: Nope. There is something else to include before I can claim *fini, tutti,* and *fait accompli.* It is an issue I am profoundly reluctant to address, but I bow to the desires of the more gregarious among our company. (Being gregarious, these people are also darned pushy, a quality we may all wish to work on a bit.) So here it is—for the pushy ones—the chapter that, when I began this book, I swore I would never write…

I can't believe I'm writing this chapter

ONCE UPON a time, there was a young man who asked his grandfather the secret of a happy, lifelong marriage. The old man solemnly replied, "Son, don't *ever* get married." As the startled young man struggled to absorb this advice, the old man added: "Unless you absolutely can't help yourself."

❖　　❖　　❖

Okay, okay. So I've told you repeatedly not to feel that you have to tell jokes. And by gum I meant it! But I meant it in a way similar to the message of the old man in this story. If you feel you should tell a joke, but aren't particularly enthusiastic about doing so, most likely you shouldn't. If, on the other hand, you are dying to tell some joke that you are certain will illustrate a teaching point beautifully, I say what's holding you up?

Having read this far, you now know that joke telling can fulfill more than one brain-based objective. You also know that you should never tell a joke to stroke your own ego, but only to have fun telling the joke—to be the Fun-Lover, not the Spotlight Grabber.

Of course, no one can take the ego completely out of joke telling. (Then again, no one can take the ego completely out of teaching!) One of the most satisfying experiences of life is making another human being's face and body contort involuntarily to expel that seventy-miles-per-hour blast of air called laughter. It's the reason comedy club hecklers exist—they're just folks who recognize the thrill we comedians are getting up there on the stage, and they're dying to have a share in the action. If you remember to focus out, you will allow your learners to do just that—share the action. They, in turn, will allow you to indulge your ego now and then by telling them jokes. They will even laugh affectionately if you bomb.

Which, however, you don't want to do too consistently. That's what this chapter is all about. I now officially cave in and reveal the Four Steps to Truly Righteous Joke Telling Every Professional Comedian Knows. Use the following information only for good, Grasshopper. . . .

Step 1: Keep It Short

Every comedian knows this inalienable fact: The longer the joke, the funnier it had better be. Go figure, maybe the average person values their time more than television producers think. In any event, Strunk and White's classic advice to writers applies equally well to comedians: *Wherever possible, choose active voice over passive, and short words over long.* For example, it's always funnier to actively say "A guy *walks*" instead of passively, "a guy *is walking*." It is also funnier to use shorter words like "a *guy has*" than, say, "a *fellow possesses*."

In the movie *The Sunshine Boys,* Walter Matthau played an aging vaudeville comedian who shares his venerable wisdom with his nephew. It went something like this: "*P* is a funny letter! *K* is another funny letter! *M? M* is *not* a funny letter!" What he was telling us was not just that hard consonants are intrinsically humorous (notice how words like *pop, butt, dog, hockey puck* just "feel" funny?), but that such consonants also tend to predominate in short, abrupt words. By the way, this is not a call to use those four-letter words some comedians hold so dear! Simply recognize the inherent comedic value of short, sharp words. "Plug," "tubby," "blip," "drag," and "racket" are funny words. "Enjoy" is not a funny word. (Yes, you're right, I myself have used it several times in this book. But never when I was trying to be funny. Good for you for noticing, however.)

Key Point: Do comedians really make such a close study of words, and even letters? Consciously or unconsciously, yes they do.

For your own study, here are a couple of jokes badly in need of shortening. See what you can do.

Trainer Practice: Shorten It Up!

Play around with these jokes. Then look at the footnotes to see if you shortened them enough.

❖ Accountants are kidded unmercifully about not having a sense of humor. Thank goodness they don't understand most of the jokes.*

❖ A lot of people are worried about their cars getting stolen these days. Yugo has come out with a new anti-theft device for their cars. They've made the Yugo emblem much larger.**

If you shortened the jokes as much as I did (or even more), pump your fist discreetly into the air before going on to Step 2.

---

* Accountants hear a lot of jokes about their lack of humor. Luckily, they don't get most of them.

** The Yugo has a new anti-theft device: They made the name bigger.

Step 2: Make It Specific

Remember from Chapter 7 how the brain likes to think in pictures? In any oral communication, concrete images are always more powerful than abstract concepts. This is doubly true in jokes: The clearer the mental picture, the funnier the joke. Note the difference in impact between these two opening lines

1. "Three women walk into a bar."

2. "Queen Elizabeth, Cindy Crawford, and Gloria Steinem walk into a bar."

In the second instance, you can mentally see the three women, and are better "set up" for something funny to happen. Now look at these two jokes:

1. "I'm afraid to fly. It's not the plane, it's the drive to the airport."

2. "I'm afraid to fly. It's not the plane, it's the drive to JFK."

I guarantee the second joke will get a better response—especially from audiences in the New York area. Which brings us to another specificity tip: Anytime you tailor your joke to your specific audience—New Yorkers, Londoners, engineers, salespeople, women, tennis players—it will get a much bigger laugh.

And now on to the next step.

Step 3: Put the Punch Line at the *End!*

Sounds obvious, doesn't it? And yet you'd be amazed. Malcolm Kushner quotes the following from a joke book written especially for speakers:

A woman was bemoaning the fact that her husband had left her for the sixth time. "Never mind," consoled the neighbor. "He'll be back." "Not this time," sobbed the wife. "He's taken his golf clubs this time."

Besides the obvious wordiness (not to mention lameness) of the joke, the force of its punch line—"he's taken his golf clubs"—is diluted when followed by the words "this time." To be even halfway funny (and this joke will never be more than that, I'm afraid), it should end, *"This time* he took his golf clubs." The golf clubs are the punch line, and the punch line is your payload. Deliver you payload—then speak nary a word more.

Here's another exercise for you.

Trainer Practice: End It with Punch

First, read this joke:

> **Question:** How many Curriculum Designers does it take to pull off a kidnapping?
>
> **Answer:** Six—five to write the ransom note and one to kidnap the victim.

Now take a stab at punching up the punch line of this joke. Check the footnote* to see how you did.

DEBRIEF
Wasn't that easy?

Step 4: . . . Pause

For some unknown reason, almost no one but professional comedians seems to know this final secret for telling great jokes. Ironically, it is incredibly simple to master, and you will find it well worth doing so. It is based on the fact that when two or more people are together *silently,* tension tends to build. (This is probably the reason everyone in an elevator stares so intently at the flashing floor numbers—we just seem uncomfortable being together without interacting.) As you now know, laughter releases tension. This means you will get a much bigger laugh if you just. . .pause. . .right before the punch line.

---

* Answer: Six—one to kidnap the victim and five to write the ransom note.

Start watching comedians on TV and see how they make use of the Golden Rule of the Pause. Then always do it yourself. You might feel a bit like a ham at first. But then, if you really love telling jokes, let's face it, you *are* a bit of a ham. Time to accept the truth about yourself. Ta-Da!

And here endeth the Lesson of the Joke. I finally broke down and did it. Are you happy now, you big ham?

Reflection Section

Without looking back, write down (or tell someone) the Four Steps to Truly Righteous Joke Telling Every Professional Comedian Knows. If you are reading this book as a member of a study group, have each member think of a joke they like, write it down (if necessary) using Steps 1 to 3, and then tell it to your group using Step 4.

....

....

....

....

....

....

....

....

We are nearly at the finish line. There is only one last issue to look at. It is of paramount importance to anyone wishing to be more humorous/creative/playful. And that, O Fearless One, is why I've left it for. . .

the best chapter in the book

IN THE BIBLE is written: "A merry heart doeth good like a medicine, but a broken spirit drieth the bones." The Talmud states: "On Judgment Day, a person will be called to account for every permissible thing he might have enjoyed—but did not." The Koran says: "He deserves Paradise who makes his companions laugh."

From the beginning, it seems, great thinkers have agreed: We are meant to have fun, to play, to laugh. Recent research suggests that laughter does indeed fulfill a biological function, affecting not only our physical health, but our mental agility as well. Chapter 5 described the findings of research suggesting that "mirthful" (as opposed to nervous or hostile) laughter reduces stress and even boosts some parts of the immune system. These preliminary conclusions seem to corroborate the now-famous anecdotal evidence of Norman Cousins, who successfully overcame a debilitating connective-tissue disease in part with daily doses of humor. Fifteen minutes of good belly laughing, he reported in *Anatomy of an Illness,* gave him two full hours of pain-free sleep.[1] Chapter 4 reported on studies showing a positive correlation between laughter and creative and cognitive thinking. Both our minds *and* our bodies seem to work significantly better when we laugh.

> **"We are what we repeatedly do. Excellence, then, is not an act, but a habit."**
>
> Aristotle, philosopher
>
> **"So is joy."**
>
> Doni Tamblyn

Following is a technique that will build your "Humor Quotient" and creativity to ever-escalating heights, while it improves your health and attitude and generally makes life a lot more worth living. I call it the One-A-Day Plan. To be honest, I stumbled upon it some years ago by pure, dumb luck. I now share it with you.

One night, while sitting in front of the TV opening my third bag of Doritos, it suddenly occurred to me that life had lost its zip. It seemed I was working only for **extrinsic** rewards—virtually everything I did came under the headings, "Make Money," "Impress People," or "Please My Folks." Meanwhile, I didn't seem to really savor much anymore, neither work nor play. I wasn't *present* in my life somehow, and it didn't feel good.

See Chap 2

It then occurred to me that when one doesn't feel good, one has two alternatives: Take something that makes you feel better, or take something that makes you stop feeling. Clearly, with my TV and snack foods I had chosen the latter. (If you haven't thought about the analgesic effects of things like TV and food, as well as things like smoking, alcohol, shopping, and so on, maybe you should!) What if I tried the former? But what was that? What *would* make me feel good, anyway? The problem was, nothing seemed to very much.

I got out a note pad and began writing down everything I had ever enjoyed in the past: keeping fresh flowers in the house; having a pet; drawing and painting; riding horses; hour-long professional massages (yes!); curling up for an hour and a half with a good book. I looked at the list and was amazed at how much time had passed, with my focus on performance, since I had done any of those things. Just thinking about them made me feel a little more buoyant. Before I knew it, other pleasant thoughts, memories, and ideas were flooding in. Soon I was feeling better than I'd felt for some time. Oh, yeah, I thought, *fun*. Fun makes you feel good. Fun with no ulterior motive. Fun with no goal. Fun for its own sake. However did I forget that?

I began to expand the list: Taking those swing dancing classes I'd been meaning to take for years; singing in an a cappella group; joining a volleyball team; living for a year in France. Feasible or not, everything that gave me a glow went on the list. Everything that made time fly went on the list. Everything I looked forward to with that little thrill of anticipation, everything I perked up just thinking about, went on the list.

Important note: Exercise did *not* go on the list.

(Nothing against exercise. It just wasn't that kind of list.)

At this moment I made what I still consider the single best decision of my life: I vowed to do one thing on that list every day. And thus did the journey begin. . . .

Day One on the One-a-Day Plan

I began to use my list religiously. I chose an activity for each day, planned for it, set the time aside, and—most challenging of all—defended that time slot! (Having fun, I discovered, is a lot like dieting: The ever-present temptation is to cheat "just this once.") Within two short weeks of daily play breaks, something new began to happen: *I now woke up every morning knowing without doubt the day would hold at least one lovely experience.*

When you are certain that good things are just around the corner, your physical energy increases as if by magic. And with positive expectation and physical energy comes motivation. With those three things—positive expectation, energy, and motivation—almost anything starts to look possible. For the first time, I began to suspect that life might after all be the extraordinary gift the poets claim, that it might hold infinite potential for surprise, pleasure, and adventure.

"Time's fun when you're having flies."
Kermit the Frog

(At this point, of course, it was only a suspicion. Don't want to move too fast with radical concepts like this. . . .)

Month One on the One-a-Day Plan

When you start enjoying your life more, the first thing you want is for everyone else to enjoy theirs, too. This is purely selfish on your part—you just want more playmates! To this end, your people skills improve as if by magic. You become a little gentler, a bit slower to take offense. One day I was making a deposit at a drive-through ATM, when suddenly the person in the car behind me leaned on his horn in one long, angry blast. I nearly jumped out of my skin and, looking back, beheld a red face contorted in rage. Gesticulating wildly, the guy bellowed, "Come ON! What's holding you up? It's just a MACHINE, lady!" (In actual fact, he phrased the thought slightly differently, but I see no need to quote him here verbatim.) My own reaction surprised me: I immediately leaned out the window and called back, "Sorry! Almost done, really. Just one minute more." I then hurried to finish my transaction so as to make the ATM available to this, my fellow traveler through life.

Now, I deeply regret to report that once upon a time I might have responded in quite another way. Perhaps by word or look I would have given this gentleman, shall we say, some useful information about himself to file for future reference. I then might have returned to my transaction and completed it just a touch more slowly. (It is so embarrassing to look back on our youthful imprudences, no?) Exiting the parking lot that day, I thought to myself, "Hm. Something has definitely changed."

Only later did I realize what it was: Feeling pretty good overall, I simply didn't wish to accept his invitation to feel bad! I didn't want to wrangle with anyone, if I could avoid it. I was quite willing to concede the small stuff, choosing my battles, so to speak. This made me finally realize what people mean who say, "Point a finger at someone else, and you've always got three fingers pointing back at you." I had always frankly considered this an empty little pop-psych platitude, but now I had to admit the truth of it: Letting little things rile you is a sure sign that something in your own life is out of balance, and you'd do far better reassessing your priorities than commenting on someone else's.

> **"Most folks are about as happy as they make up their minds to be."**
> Abraham Lincoln, American president

Month Six on the One-a-Day Plan

When you insist on having fun on a regular basis, after a while you start to develop a habit of happiness, instinctively gravitating toward those experiences that feed you, and away from those that don't. At a certain point, for example, I found I was prioritizing time differently. Formerly I had lived by the credo: "Do the unpleasant work first and get it out of the way, then do the fun stuff." (Sound familiar, by any chance?) One day I decided, Nope. Fun stuff first. And to my astonishment, I quickly discovered this works better! So well, in fact, that I began to refer to the technique of leaving your crummy tasks till the last reasonable moment as "Sane Procrastination."

There are many excellent reasons to use Sane Procrastination.

First, those chores you find relatively tedious—maybe filing, or bookkeeping, writing timelines, or comparing long distance carriers—tend to drain you. Meanwhile those you find meaningful—brainstorming, doing a PowerPoint design, mentoring a colleague, building a model airplane, whatever—energize you. This means that if you work on the fun jobs first, you will find yourself attacking the tedious ones with more vitality, which also usually means you'll get through them more quickly, and do a more competent job.

The second reason to use Sane Procrastination is that if you're a true "Type A" (or, to be blunt, a perfectionist) there is no end to the number of crummy, lousy, boring jobs that can keep you from what you truly love.

> **❝One of the greatest labor-saving inventions of today is tomorrow.❞**
>
> Vincent T. Foss,
> famous procrastinator

"Whoops," you'll say, "can't do the fun stuff yet—haven't hand-washed my shoelaces. Then there are the tooth brushes to align...." At this rate, a person can go to his grave without ever once playing "Group Count" from Chapter 4. A tragedy indeed!

The third reason to use Sane Procrastination is that in leaving your crummy chores till the last reasonable moment you create a deadline for yourself. As the adage goes, every job expands to fill the time available. This is doubly true of boring tasks. With time to spare, you will most assuredly dawdle. The best antidote I know to dawdling is a deadline. This may be only an **extrinsic** motivator, but when it comes to work you dislike, it's probably the best motivator you're going to get.

See
Chap 2

The last and maybe best reason to use Sane Procrastination is that sometimes—if you're really lucky—the lousy stuff disappears!

Yes, this does legitimately happen! Not often, but sometimes. Maybe you find you don't have to start that pointless-seeming project after all because you just got a transfer to another department, yee-hah! Or maybe the IRS suddenly discontinues that irksome form you've always had to fill out—who knows why, and indeed who really cares? Maybe your personal priorities simply shifted, and that task you considered of top importance last week looks like a poor return on investment this week. The fact is, in this random universe priorities are often like the waves of the sea, rising up one moment and falling away just as quickly. This is a fact we constantly seem to forget.

Month Twelve on the One-a-Day Plan

If there was only one reason to make time for fun every day, it would decidedly be this: It fosters within you a deep and abiding conviction of your own pricelessness. You begin to feel you must have value—after all, someone keeps bringing you these wonderful gifts every day. And the gifts are not meant to help you lose weight, or increase your income potential, or in any other way make you more "worthy." Their sole purpose is to make you happy. And that feels very much like love, my friend.

Without knowing quite how it had happened, I suddenly found that I was spending the majority of each day on tasks I enjoyed. Marsha Sinetar[2] has said that if you do what you love the money will follow. There is really nothing mystical about this advice. In doing what you love, you essentially position yourself professionally. Example: In the introduction to this book, I described my experiences as an instructor coordinator for a California traffic school. What I didn't mention was that I started out as an instructor, in what was meant to be a temporary, part-time job supplementing my income as a struggling comedian and commercial actor. No one was more surprised than I when I found I

> **"When you are genuinely interested in one thing it will always lead to something else."**
> Eleanor Roosevelt, American First Lady

loved teaching traffic safety to my "violators!" It was uniquely satisfying to use my performance and comedy skills to help people accomplish something bothersome but necessary—and to accomplish it well. I poured myself into that job, simply because it interested me. I sought out progressive learning techniques, studied training design and brain theory. The next thing I knew, my company HumorRules® was born. To date, I have traveled a good part of the world as a speaker and trainer, worked with a number of multinational corporations, and published two books on my topic.

When asked by his students at Sarah Lawrence College how to find their life's path, Joseph Campbell answered, "Follow your bliss." From my experience, and that of others who insist on fun, he was right on the money. No one knows why you were given your particular talents and loves. But I'm willing to bet you got them for a reason. You need to enjoy them as often as you possibly can.

One day I told a friend, "I think I may have discovered the single easiest self-improvement regimen in the world: Have more fun. This stuff is astonishing—it boosts your energy, perks up your attitude, improves your work habits, changes your eating habits, and clears up your skin. You've got to try it!"

"Life is short. Eat dessert first."

Bumper sticker

"What a nice thought," she replied. "But I have children. People with children cannot enjoy every day of their lives. It's just not an option. Thank you for the thought, though."

Everybody's a comedian, I thought wryly. Then I had a flash of inspiration.

"Wait!" I said. "You want them to enjoy every day of *their* lives, right?" Naturally she nodded. "So who," I continued craftily, "will model this life skill for them, if not their own mother?"

Mothers are such pushovers. You can always get them with guilt.

My friend tried it. And predictably she ran into a problem, which she described thusly: "You can set aside your hour of time. You can fill the tub with bubble bath, you can get your good book, you can even put a new lock on the bathroom door. None of this matters. When you have children, there is one little word you will hear on the other side of that door every five minutes: 'Mom.' And that one word can open any door better than a medieval battering ram."

I must confess, I was stymied.

"Fortunately," she added, smiling, "there is a magical, three-word answer to that."

"What is it?" I asked.

"'Is anybody bleeding?'"

Make no mistake. In claiming your bliss daily, you will fly in the face of conventional wisdom. Among other things, this "wisdom" dictates that good people don't put themselves first. But this wisdom is clearly absurd. Even Mother Theresa, whose life was devoted to helping the poorest of the poor, had to first sustain herself, else she could never have carried on as long as she did. Those we love best can sometimes call on us for sacrifices that, in depleting us, will ultimately dispossess them. Do your own loved ones a favor: Teach them better. In modeling a healthy self-interest, you will give them permission to do the same—to value their own lives, to set things up for themselves so that they look forward to each day, ultimately to feel glad that they were born. What better gift could you give anyone than that?

Be strong, O Fearless One. Today as a person you are making your own life more fun for yourself. Tomorrow as a teacher you are adding to the whole world's bliss. Not bad for a day's work.

"Our deepest fear is not that we are inadequate. Our deepest fear is that we are powerful beyond measure. It is our light, not our darkness, that most frightens us. We ask ourselves, who are we to be brilliant, gorgeous, talented and fabulous? Actually, who are you not to be? Your playing small doesn't serve the world. There is nothing enlightened about shrinking so other people won't feel insecure around you. . . . As we let our light shine, we unconsciously give other people permission to do the same. As we are liberated from our own fear, our presence automatically liberates others."

Nelson Mandela,
1994 inaugural address

endnotes

CHAPTER 2

1. Conversation with Eric Jensen, January 2002.

2. For a global listing of branches, visit the Theatresports Web site at www.intl-theatresports.ab.ca.

3. Pat Wolfe, *Brain Matters: Translating Research Into Classroom Practice* (Alexandria, Va.: Association for Supervision & Curriculum Development, 2001).

CHAPTER 4

1. William J.J. Gordon, *Synectics* (New York: Harper & Row, 1961).

2. Alice Isen, et al., "The Influence of Positive Affect on Clinical Problem Solving." *Medical Decision Making* (July-September 1991).

3. Richard Metzger, et al., "Worry Changes Decision Making: The Effects of Negative Thoughts on Cognitive Processing," *Journal of Clinical Psychology* (January 1990).

4. Martin E.P. Seligman, *Learned Optimism* (New York: Alfred A. Knopf, 1991).

CHAPTER 5

1. Colin Rose, *Accelerated Learning for the 21st Century* (New York: Dell Publishing, 1997).

2. David Keirsey and Marilyn Bates. *Please Understand Me: Character and Temperament Types.* (Del Mar, Calif: Prometheus Nemesis Book Company, 1978.)

CHAPTER 6

1. The ways in which we humans can signal lack of confidence are multifarious and amazing. If you are a woman wondering why you don't seem to convey the competence you know you have, you might be very interested in Gale Evan's book, *Play Like a Man, Win Like a Woman* (New York: Broadway Books, 2000).

2. Malcolm Kushner, *The Light Touch: How to Use Humor for Business Success* (New York: Simon & Schuster, 1991). Ninety-minute audiotape.

3. David Keirsey and Marilyn Bates. *Please Understand Me: Character and Temperament Types.* (Del Mar, Calif: Prometheus Nemesis Book Company, 1978.)

CHAPTER 7

1. Trainer's Warehouse (Telephone: 1-800-299-3770). *Web site: www.train erswarehouse.com.*

2. Peggy Noonan, *What I Saw at the Revolution: A Political Life in the Reagan Era* (New York: Ballantine Books, 1990).

3. Bill Moyers, *The Public Mind,* Part 3: "Imitating the News." Video series aired 1998.

4. Nancy Margulies, *Mapping Inner Space: Learning and Teaching Mind Mapping* (Flagstaff, Ariz: Zephyr Press, 1991).

CHAPTER 8

1. Daniel Goleman, *Emotional Intelligence* (New York: Bantam Books, 1995).

2. Ellen Sullins, "Emotional Contagion Revisisted: Effects of Social Comparison and Expressive Style on Mood Convergence." *Personality and Social Psychology Bulletin,* vol. 17, issue 2, p. 166.

CHAPTER 9

1. Alan Downs, *Corporate Executions* (New York: AMACOM, 1995).

2. One juggling supply store that sells scarves at a reasonable price is Brian Dubé, Inc. in New York. You can find the Dubé store online at *www.dube.com.* Pricing changes occasionally, but there is bulk discounting.

3. David Keirsey and Marilyn Bates. *Please Understand Me: Character and Temperament Types.* (Del Mar, Calif: Prometheus Nemesis Book Company, 1978.)

4. Trainer's Warehouse (Telephone: 1-800-299-3770). Web site: *www.train erswarehouse.com.*

CHAPTER 10

1. Taken from Doni Tamblyn and Sharyn Weiss, *The Big Book of Humorous Training Games* (New York: McGraw-Hill, 2000). Reprinted with permission.

CHAPTER 12

1. Norman Cousins, *Anatomy of an Illness as Perceived by the Patient* (New York: W.W. Norton & Co., 1979).

2. Marsha Sinetar, *Do What You Love, the Money Will Follow: Discovering Your Right Livelihood* (New York: Paulist Press, 1986).

bibliography

BOOKS

Bennet, Hal Zina and Susan J. Sparrow. *Follow Your Bliss.* New York: Avon Books, 1990.

Cousins, Norman. *Anatomy of an Illness As Perceived by the Patient.* New York: W.W. Norton & Company, 1979.

Csikszentmihalyi, Mihaly. *Flow: The Psychology of Optimal Experience,* 1st edition. New York: Harper and Row, 1990.

De Bono, Edward. *Six Thinking Hats.* Boston: Little, Brown, 1986.

De Bono, Edward. *Serious Creativity.* New York: The McQuaing Group, 1992.

Goleman, Daniel. *Emotional Intelligence.* New York: Bantam Books, 1995.

Goleman, Daniel. *Working with Emotional Intelligence.* New York: Bantam Books, 1998.

Jensen, Eric. *Sizzle and Substance.* San Diego, Calif.: The Brain Store, 1999.

Jensen, Eric. *Super Teaching.* San Diego, Calif.: The Brain Store, 1998.

Johnstone, Keith. *Impro: Improvisation and the Theatre.* New York: Theatre Arts Books, Routledge, 1998.

Johnstone, Keith. *Impro for Storytellers.* New York: Theatre Arts Books, Routledge, 1999.

Keirsey, David and Marilyn Bates. *Please Understand Me: Character and Temperament Types.* Del Mar, Calif.: Prometheus Nemesis Book Company, 1978.

Keirsey, David and Marilyn Bates. *Please Understand Me II: Temperament, Character, and Intelligence.* Del Mar, Calif.: Prometheus Nemesis Book Company, 1998.)

Kushner, Malcolm. *Public Speaking for Dummies.* Foster City, Calif.: IDG Books Worldwide, 1999.

Kohn, Alfie. *Punished by Rewards: The Trouble with Gold Stars, Incentive Plans, A's, Praise, and Other Bribes.* Boston, Mass.: Houghton-Mifflin, 1999.

LeDoux, Joseph. *The Emotional Brain: The Mysterious Underpinnings of Emotional Life.* New York: Simon & Schuster, 1998.

Margulies, Nancy. *Mapping Inner Space: Learning and Teaching Visual Mapping.* Flagstaff, Ariz.: Zephyr Press, 1991.

Rose, Colin. *Accelerated Learning for the Twenty-first Century.* New York: Dell Publishing, 1997.

Seligman, Martin. *Learned Optimism.* New York: Alfred A. Knopf, 1991.

Sinetar, Marsha. *Do What You Love, the Money Will Follow: Discovering Your Right Livelihood.* New York: Paulist Press, 1986.

Tamblyn, Doni and Sharyn Weiss. *The Big Book of Humorous Training Games.* New York: McGraw-Hill, 2000.

Wolfe, Pat. *Brain Matters: Translating Research Into Classroom Practice.* Association for Supervision & Curriculum Development, 2001.

AUDIO TAPES

Kushner, Malcolm. *The Light Touch: How to Use Humor for Business Success.* New York: Simon & Schuster, 1991. Ninety minutes.

RESOURCES

Improvisation classes

International Theatresports™. *Web site: www.intl-theatresports.ab.ca*

Music

The LIND Institute

P.O. Box 14487, San Francisco CA 94114

Telephone: (800) 462-3766

(This group puts out collections of music chosen specifically to calm, energize, inspire, or engage learners.)

Trainer's Warehouse
Telephone: 1-800-299-3770
Web site: *www.trainerswarehouse.com*
(They have two collections of royalty-free music, "Tunes for Trainers" and "Jazzy Tunes for Trainers." These include cool stuff you won't find anywhere else, like Game Show theme songs and tunes announcing breaks. I personally find the humor in the break tune lyrics a bit inconsistent; still, there's lots of usable stuff there.)

Art

Blake, Quentin and John Cassidy. *Drawing for the Artistically Undiscovered.* Palo Alto, Calif.: Klutz, 1999.

Brandt, Richard C. *Flip Charts: How to Draw Them and How to Use Them.* San Francisco: Jossey-Bass/Pfeiffer, 1989.

Westcott, Jean and Jennifer Hammond Landau. *A Picture's Worth 1,000 Words: A Workbook for Visual Communicators.* San Francisco: Jossey-Bass/Pfeiffer, 1996.

Humor and Anecdotes

Braude, Jacob M. *Braude's Treasury of Wit and Humor for All Occasions.* Englewood Cliffs, N.J.: Prentice Hall, 1991.

Griffith, Joe. *Speaker's Library of Business Stories, Anecdotes, and Humor.* New York: Barnes & Noble Books, 1990.

Malcom Kushner's Web site: *www.kushnergroup.com/*

ORGANIZATIONS AND ASSOCIATIONS

The HUMOR Project
480 Broadway, Suite 210
Saratoga Springs, N.Y., 12866-2288
Telephone: (518) 587-8770
Web site: *www.humorproject.com/*

(An international organization that brings together people from many industries and walks of life, all of whom share a belief in the value of humor. Get on their mailing list: They send out a super catalogue of humor products, and have a yearly conference in Saratoga Springs, which is a charming town to visit when the weather's good.)

The International Society for Humor Studies
Web site: *www.uniduesseldorf.de/WWW/MathNat/Ruch/Secretary Page.html*
(This group focuses on academic research on the effects of humor on memory, pain management, social relations, health, and a host of other things. They put out a journal, *Humor,* and hold yearly conferences to share information. Vocabulary required.)

The Association of Applied and Therapeutic Humor
951 W. Camelback Rd. Ste. 445
Phoenix AZ 85015
Telephone: 602-995-1454
Web site: *www.AATH.org*
(The purpose of this organization is to educate health care professionals and lay audiences about the values and therapeutic uses of humor and laughter. Although most of their membership is comprised of practicing health professionals, they welcome anyone who is interested in learning more about the benefits of therapeutic humor. They put out the *AATH Newsletter.*)

anatomy of a
creative learning
module

one-day workshop on humor
and brain-based learning

(Note: The following is a guide, not a prescription. Use any techniques that feel right for you, and discard any that don't. Also, feel free to steal jokes! Most of all, notice how organized you must be in terms of procedures and timing in order to keep order in your Laughing Classroom. Challenge is an intrinsic motivator—enjoy it! And remember one thing: As you practice Creative Learning, these techniques will require less conscious thought on your part, appearing more and more spontaneously in both your design and delivery.)

Ideal Room Setup: Nonfluorescent lighting; good climate control; Ionizer; background music ("Four Seasons," Vivaldi). Five tables set spaciously apart, five to seven places per table, each set with three-ring binders with colored learning materials, new pens. At center of each table: jug of unchilled water, glasses, bananas, apples, and oranges. Posters around room with captions like "Downtime Lets Us Make Meaning," "Emotion Makes It Real," etc. (*Objectives: Eliminate stress; manage state [curiosity through novelty]; enrichment through nonconscious learning, feed the brain; multi-path learning; create attention with color.*)

9:00 – INTRODUCTION

[Presenter enters and stands at the front of the room silently for a few moments, making brief eye contact with individual students (i.e., rather than "mass contact," sweeping eyes over the group). Lets hubbub subside before beginning. Takes a big drink of water to model hydrating the brain.]

"Well, good morning all. How are you doing? Yes? Glad to hear it.

"I would like to start today off by reciting for you the first-day speech of my eighth-grade math teacher. I will never forget that speech. It went something like this:

> You will not be late to this class. If you are late three times, you will get THE STRAP! (Whack a ruler on desk.) You will not whisper in class. You will not pass notes. You will not chew gum. If you are caught chewing gum at ANY time, you get THE STRAP! (Whack) You will do all assigned homework. I will not always ask to see your homework. If I do ask to see your homework, and you have not done it, you get THE STRAP! (Whack)

"He then proceeded to discuss negative versus positive numeric values:

> Values change EVERYTHING! They change your APPROACH! They change OUTCOMES! For instance: when you subtract a positive from a positive, you get a SMALLER NUMBER! When you subtract a negative from a negative, what do you get...THOMPSON?

"Good old Thompson, bless his heart, stammered out the only answer he could think of: 'The strap?'"

(*Objectives: Rapport [personal, humorous story]; eliminate stress; engage emotions; show relevance through story-telling.*)

"The preceding is *NOT* an example of Brain-Compatible Learning! One of the very first imperatives of BCL is to eliminate threat from the learning environment. Got that? And now let's see a show of hands: How many find studying scientific and biological research really fun? [Show of hands.] How many find it a little intimidating? [Show of hands.] How many hate the stuff? [Show of hands.] Did anyone not raise their hand? If not, why not? [Take comments.] (*Objectives: Rapport through flocking; feedback.*) Okay, notice we've got people here from a range of starting points. We're going to work today in ways that will allow each of you, from wherever you start, to learn the information in this course. (*Objective: Remove threat.*) Is that really possible with such a diverse group? (*Objective: Mental stimulation through questions.*) You will find out that it is. (*Objective: Affirmation.*)

"Let me tell you, you could spend a lifetime studying any *one* aspect of brain-based learning—and some people do. We're going to distill this incredibly multifarious topic down to five manageable (*Objective: Remove threat.*)—and crucial (*Objective: Relevance.*)—issues. Here's what we'll learn today:"

Overhead: Course outline with "You Are Here" dot placed at starting point. (*Objectives: Relevance; curiosity about the day's curriculum.*)

1. *The brain's uniqueness*

2. *Threat or high stress*

3. *Cycles, rhythms, and making measning: attention*

4. *Emotions and states*

5. *LTP (long-term potentiation of information, a.k.a., long-term memory)*

"Multifarious as this stuff may be, it's easy for brainy people like you. (*Objective: Affirmation.*) That's because it's so gosh-darned interesting. At least, I think it is. I don't know; does anyone else find learning interesting? [Show of hands] I thought you might, being teachers and all. (*Objectives: Managing states; rapport.*) You know, even if we all had the same starting point, our paths to learning would still be unique to each of us. Because each of our brains is wired differently. A foundational principle of BCL is to recognize this fact—that each of our brains is... [Hand to ear, expectant look. Students: "*Wired differently.*"] So true. Gosh, you guys are good....

"Yep, each of our brains is wired differently. And so we have to design training that accommodates each brain's needs. One good way to do that is to design *experiential* learning. Today you will learn many techniques by experiencing them. I'll ask you to take part in a multitude of learning activities. On the surface, some of these may seem odd to you—some maybe even silly. I will ask you to keep an open mind and try them out. Of course, you do not have to take part in anything you object to for any reason. Hey, it's not like I can flunk you for it. That's right. You're not in school anymore. You're an adult—you take seminars! Now turn to the person next to you and say, 'It's good to be an adult!' (*Objectives: Affirmation; choice; flocking; also humor to open them to next statement.*)

"Seriously, having said all this, I strongly recommend that you *do* take part in all of today's activities. Why? Because you'll have more physical energy and mental alertness. And because the best way to learn is to do. And because I will of, course, explain the brain-based principle behind each activity to you as we go along! So let's get started.

"Now please take 2.5 minutes to write out the questions you most want to have answered today. Ready? Go." (*Objectives: Von Restorff Effect; personal relevancy.*)

Music: Beethoven's Piano Concerto #5 (*Objective: Mental primer.*)

Flip Chart: Blank

"Okay, what questions do you have that you want answered today? [Write out questions.] We'll make sure to answer all of these today and/or show you where to get more information after today. Of course, your amazing brain will think of more questions as the day progresses. Be sure to ask them! (*Objectives: Affirmation, choice, feedback.*)

"As the leader for today, it's my job to juggle two conflicting imperatives: 1) let everyone get what they need from the course, and 2) make sure we end on time! Thank you, thank you. No, please—hold your applause. (*Objective: Relieve stress about overly long learning modules.*) To accomplish this, I will divide today's questions into three categories:

❖ General Interest Unplanned

❖ General Interest Planned

❖ Specific Interest

"*General Interest Unplanned* means I wasn't planning to talk about your question today, but I know lots of people here would like to know the answer to it. I will answer that question immediately. *General Interest Planned* means lots of people here would like to hear the answer to your question, *and* I was already planning to discuss it. You'll probably hear me answer it very briefly and then say, 'Hang on, we're building up to it.' *Specific Interest* means your question relates pretty specifically to you and your work. That's when you'll hear me say, 'Let's talk about it at break.'

"Okay, please take a deep breath. Sit back. Stand. Stretch out a little. Let's do some gentle aerobics. I'll lead this time; you'll lead next time. [Lead aerobics.] (*Objectives: Mood lifter, Ziegarnick Effect.*) And now please turn to the person closest to you and tell them one thing we've done already today that you think might be brain-based, and why you think so. If you don't know why, guess! Take 2 3/4 minutes. Ready? Go." (*Objectives: Emotional engagement through problem solving without instructions; questions; downtime; flocking.*)

[Blow train whistle to signal end of exercise.] (*Objectives: Novelty; attention.*)

"By the way, since aerobics were the last thing we did before this exercise, I'm willing to bet lots of you mentioned aerobics. How many mentioned aerobics? [Show of hands; laughter.] And since the story of my eighth-grade math teacher was the first, lots of you probably remembered that. How many mentioned the story of my math teacher? [Show of hands.] You have just learned something about learning: We remember best what's at the *beginning* and at the *end* of any module. So where might you put important learning material? At the. . . [Chant: *"Beginning"*] and the. . . [Chant: *"End!"*] of modules. Nice. Very nice. No flies on you, I can see that. It's going to be quite a day. (**Objectives:** *Personal involvement through chants, questions; affirmation.*) Okay, before sitting down, turn to your partner and say, 'We're obviously going to learn a lot today!'" (**Objective:** *Affirmation.*)

9:30 – THE BRAIN'S UNIQUENESS

Overhead: "You Are Here" [Move dot to "Your Unique Brain".]

[Using preprinted binder notes, give twenty-minute lecture. After each ten minutes, do a quick review using chants, like: "Each person's brain is wired. . ." *"Differently."* "That's because the brain is an. . ." *"Adaptive organ."* "Yes! It produces dendrites in response to your. . ." *"Environment."* "And your. . ." "Experience." "Thank you. So to expect all learners to move at the same pace is. . ." *"Unrealistic."* "Okay, I'll take that. Because it's also. . ." *"Brain antagonistic."* "Yes! Isn't it, though. By the way, humor involves the creative act of. . ." *"Making new connections."* "Which means it can promote. . ." *"Dendrite growth!"* "Yeah! Thank you very much."]

9:50 – "Okay, would you please take a deep breath? There you go. That's called 'oxygen.' You may have encountered it before. Did you know it's one of the brain's favorite fuels? Go ahead and stretch a little. And will you now please stand up? We're going to do something called Cross Laterals. You'll find out exactly what they're for later." (**Objective:** *Creating a state of curiosity.*) [Lead two cross lateral exercises.] (**Objectives:** *Physicality; creating attention.*) "Thank you. Now, before sitting down, please turn to the person next to you and say, 'That woke my brain up!' (**Objective:** *Affirmation.*) Thank you. Please have a seat."

9:55 – THREAT AND HIGH STRESS

Overhead: "You Are Here" [Move dot to "Threat and High Stress".]

[Before discussing, give learners 2 and seven-eigths minutes to brainstorm with others at their tables about which techniques already used today might have been specifically aimed at reducing stress. Someone from each table stands and tells the class one thing their group noticed. Allow answers to springboard you into explanations of choice, affirmations, starting and ending on time, music, physicality, humor. (*Objectives: Flocking; personal interaction and involvement.*)

Discuss issues of threat and high stress: neural response of; environmental causes of; further strategies to minimize. Note that learners will experience one big threat-reducing strategy—teams—in the last quarter of the day.]

10:15 – [Conduct review with Finish-the Sentence Ball Toss.]

10:20 – Flip Chart: Questions. "Have we answered any? Got any others?"

10:30 – [Give learners 5 and three-quarters minutes to write about what they've learned so far today.]

"Okay, you just experienced downtime, allowing your brain to make meaning of new information. You'll find out why that's so important when we come back from break. (*Objective: Creating a state of curiosity.*) Let's take 15.33 minutes. Two minutes before the break is over I'll put on a tape of the song, 'We Will Rock You.' That's how you'll know it's time to start coming back. When the music ends, you'll be at your table. Right? [*"Right!"*] Thank you. Enjoy your break."

10:35–10:50 15 MINUTE BREAK

10:50 – CYCLES, RHYTHMS, AND MAKING MEANING: ATTENTION

Overhead: "You Are Here" [Move dot to "Attention".]

"Something every trainer must keep in mind is that the brain is capable of 100 percent attention only 25 percent of the time. That's right. You thought it was just you. Nope—everybody's that way! Here's how it works:"

[Explain, using binder notes: basics of cycles and rhythms; value of downtime; applications. As a way of review throughout lecture, have attendees stand whenever they think they remember a technique used so far this morning to facilitate making meaning, heightening attention, or review.]

"Please take a few minutes of downtime right now to write about what we've just discussed, with this question in mind: At what points in a learning module is it *imperative* for the teacher to create attention?" (Answer: openings, summaries, and key points.)

11:15 – "Who has remembered to take a deep breath in the last twenty minutes? Anyone feel like stretching? Go ahead. Then have a little water. Ahh. Your brain *likes* you." (*Objective: Ziegnarick break.*)

11:20 – EMOTIONS AND STATES
Overhead: "You Are Here"—[Move dot to "States."]

"Take a deep breath. This is the most important topic of the day. I'm only going to say this once. Are you ready?

"Okay, check out how you feel right now! What is your body doing? What's going on in your mind? This is a state of full attention—you're ready to spring on the information. Let's call this the 'Panther State.' Anytime I say, 'Panther State' today, do what you just did. Got it?"

[Discuss states, using binder notes: Mind/body nature of states; types of states.]

11:35 – *Activity:* Learners mimic seven most common participant states: disappointment; curiosity/anticipation; fear; confusion; apathy/boredom; self-convincer; frustration. (*Objective: Kinesthetic learning.*)

"Okay, Panther State! (*Objective: Managing states.*) How do we look when we are in each of these states? Well, our learners look this way, too! In other words, they are constantly signaling when they need a state change. Question: What can we do to manage our learners' states? Hint: I have used a number of state-management techniques today. Okay, take 5 and one-third minutes to write down your thoughts." (*Objectives: Downtime; making meaning.*)

"All right, you just had some more of that highly fruitful downtime. Now let's hear what you wrote."

11:45 – [Ball toss between participants as they give the answers they came up with. With particularly rich ideas, say, "Panther State!" and make them repeat. (*Objectives: Multipathway learning re states; attention; physicality; celebration of good ideas.*) Do a quick review using Chants.]

11:55 – *Flip Chart:* Questions. "What did we answer? Any other questions?

"We'll stop in a minute for lunch. At exactly 1:03 I'll start playing 'We Will Rock You,' and you know you have two minutes to...what? [*"Get to our seats."*] Why, that's exactly right. Before we go, please turn to the person nearest you and say, 'The brain works in amazing ways!' (*Objective: Affirmation.*) Okay, thank you and have a good lunch."

12:00–1:05 LUNCH

Ideal Room Setup: Fresh water on tables, with bowl of peanuts, pecans. One cardboard nameplate on each table.

Music: Haydn's *Toy Symphony*

[Choose someone to lead a gentle, three-minute stretching session.]

Music: Tchaikovsky's *Piano Concerto*

Overhead: "You Are Here"—[Move dot to "Emotions".]

Overhead: [Tell story of "Elliot," whose neo-cortex and so-called emotional brain could no longer "talk" to each other. (*Objective: Relevancy through story-telling.*) Discuss using binder notes: the importance of emotions; the six primary emotions; appropriate and inappropriate emotions, and emotional literacy; enthusiasm; synchrony (pacing); mood lifters.]

1:25 – *Exercise:* (9 and seven-eighths minutes) Pacing— "Talk to the person next to you about what you had for lunch. And while you're talking, pace each other. Go!" [Debrief.]

"Many of us tend to feel uncomfortable even with some of our *own* emotions! In particular, many of us have come to believe that anger, fear, sadness, and disgust are *ipso facto* bad. But all emotions are real, and human, and as such cannot be bad. We simply have to know how to manage them. Just as you can manage your learners' states, you can also manage their emotions, and ultimately help them to manage their own. Want to practice a little Emotional Management right now? Okay, let's do it.

"One of the first steps to emotional management is also one of the first steps to being truly creative, playful, and humorous:

"*Allow imperfection!*

"That's right. It's called tolerance. How many have heard of it? Okay, here's another question: How many here have ever made a mistake? [Show of hands, laughter.] How about that? Has anybody here made *more* than one? [Show of hands.] Hm. How many expect to make at least *one* more mistake before you die? [Show of hands.] So, let me get this right, none of us here are perfect. Yet how many of us are sometimes a bit perfectionistic? [Show of hands.] Hm. Of course, it's a great thing to want to do your very best. But how many would say that perfectionism has ever led you to have rigid expectations? Let's play a few games to help us lose our intolerant, perfectionistic tendencies."

Music: Theme from *Exodus; Peter and the Wolf;* Beethoven's *Egmont Overture;* or anything upbeat by Handel, Tchaikovsky, Brahms, Schubert, Mendelssohn.

1:40 – *Activities:*

❖ Clown Bow; Numbers Horseshoe (Acknowledge the Bomb)

❖ "So Sue Me" Ritual; One Word Instructions (Cut Each Other Some Gosh-Darned Slack)

"Very nice work. [Mention a few highlights of the games.] Mary kept calling out her own number in Numbers Horseshoe—but she always did the Clown Bow *so well!* Etc. Now everybody give yourselves a hand for being so relaxed, spontaneous, and—most of all—tolerant! *Yes!* [Lead applause.] (***Objective:*** *Celebration.*)

"We've learned that we have lots of unworkable ideas—and sometimes some 'unworkable' emotions. And that that's okay if we cut ourselves and others some gosh-darned. . ." (*"Slack!"*) "Yes! And also by. . ." (*"Acknowledging the bomb."*) "Yes. Thank you *very* much.

2:10 – "And now take seven minutes to discuss unworkable emotions that might show up in any learning environment, and possible ways to manage those emotions."

[Attendees offer their ideas using Ball Toss. Possible answers: Unworkable emotions—fear, anger. To manage—modeling enthusiasm; synchrony; pacing; acknowledging the bomb; affirmations; active listening; humor; physicality.]

2:25 – ***Overhead:*** Questions. "What did we answer? Got any more?

"Okay, we'll break for fifteen minutes. Come back when you hear 'We Will Rock You.' But wait—before we go for our break, look around your table. Because when you come back, something will be different, and I'm going to ask you what it is. Okay, enjoy your break—outside, please." (Note: This is a gag to make them expect something will be done to the room while they are out of it. In fact, nothing in the room will be altered. ***Objectives:*** *Create state of curiosity; lighten with humor.*)

2:35–2:50 15 MINUTE BREAK

Overhead: "You Are Here"—[Move dot to "LTP".]

"Welcome back. Look around you—what's different? You don't know? What? I can't believe this. What's different is that the people at your table are. . .*your team!* That's right! Slap yourselves on the foreheads. Now turn to them and say, 'I *thought* I knew you from somewhere!'"

[Briefly explain some benefits of team learning: flocking, downtime, multi-modal learning, and peer feedback.]

Music: Mozart's Violin Concerto #4

2:45 – [Have participants choose leaders, make up team names (write on tent cards), create their own team cheer.] (***Objectives:*** *Interactive, experiential learning about flocking, peer feedback.*)

3:00 – [Explain LTP: visual memory; Von Restorff Effect and humor; repetition; especially, once again, the importance of review.]

"Now let's try a particularly good way to review today's curriculum. Your teams will now compete against each other in the challenging and venerable game of *Jeopardy.* At the end of this competition, some lucky team will take home. . . *FABULOUS PRIZES!* Yes, you heard right, fabulous prizes. Unfortunately, I can't tell you exactly what they are, since it's a closely guarded secret. You'll just have to compete for them without knowing. But I assure you, they are *plenty* fabulous! So are you ready to lie, cheat, maim, and kill to win them? [*"Yes!!"*] Then you're out of the game. Only sportsmanlike behavior will be tolerated here, you brainy thugs. Okay, now that we've got that clear, let's go. . . ."

3:10 – *Exercise:* Jeopardy

[Each team has fourteen minutes to go over one of today's five topics and generate five questions about it. They must, of course, phrase the questions in the form of answers. Write each on 8 ½ x 11 paper. Have *Jeopardy* board at front, into which answers can be fitted with blue cards covering them. Instead of dollar amounts being printed on the cards, as in the real *Jeopardy* (the teams won't play for graduating amounts of money, but simply for correct answers), you can have illustrations of a brain, a smiling mouth, or anything you like. Or you can leave them blank. Proceed to play. When teams get an answer right, they give their team cheer. The winning team members receive foam rubber brains, stuffed fabric bananas—it doesn't really matter. Actually, the weirder the better.] (***Objectives:*** *Review; flocking; celebration.*)

3:45 – *Overhead:* Questions. "Have all questions been answered today? Any last ones?

"Thank you, ladies and gentlemen. And now will you make some final notes in your journals, and then fill out your evaluations while I prepare for the awards ceremony."

Music: Handel's Water Music

3:50 – AWARDS CEREMONY

Music: Queen's "We Are the Champions"

[Hand out certificates of completion; also special awards, like "Most Mistakes (Summa cum laude Creative Thinker)," "Best Slack-Cutter," "Best Clown Bow," "Best Pitching Arm" (for Ball Toss), whatever you like.] (*Objectives: Review; celebration.*)

Brief Closing Address: Finish with whole class yelling, "We are super trainers! *Yes!*"

Music: "We Are the Champions," to end.

❖　❖　❖

Questions?

Do you have a question about using humor in your own work? Mail, fax, or e-mail your query. Doni Tamblyn will answer it personally—and might even include it in a future publication! Send your quesiton to:

Q&A
c/o HumorRules
P.O. Box 22575
Philadelphia, PA 19110
Fax: (215) 732-7674
e-mail: tamblyn@humorrules.com

index

about the author

Doni Tamblyn is president of HumorRules®, a Philadelphia-based training and consulting firm that helps organizations to attract quality employees and build their skills quickly.

In 1979, Doni began writing and performing comedy for stage, radio, and television. A former member of the American Film, Television, and Radio Actors Union, she has appeared in numerous print and radio ads, and on local television and radio entertainment shows. As a stage actor and singer, she founded two award-winning musical comedy groups, Sirens and The Dinettes, and was a member of the San Francisco Bay Area Theatresports Workshop Players. Her full-length play *Looks* won an award in the 1998 *Writer's Digest* Writing Competition.

Doni's experience in training began in 1989, when she was hired as a professional comedian to breathe life into state-sanctioned classes for traffic violators. To her surprise, what she considered a purely temporary "day job" became a fascinating exploration into the nature of learning. She began studying adult learning theories, with a particular emphasis on progressive techniques like Accelerative Learning and Brain-Compatible Learning. As instructor coordinator for one statewide traffic school, she standardized training for both the classes and the professional comedians she hired to teach them. Attendee ratings subsequently rose by some 20 percent, and the school was one of a select group chosen for a study by the California Department of Motor Vehicles on effective teaching techniques.

Doni founded HumorRules in 1993. Since her entry into the corporate world, Doni's writing has appeared in business journals including *Training* magazine, *Asia PR Alert* (a Hong Kong periodical), *AHP Perspective*, and other periodicals. She was lead author of *The Big Book of Humorous Training Games* (McGraw-Hill, 2000). HumorRules' client list includes such notable corporations as Chevron, Wells Fargo Bank, Bristol-Meyers Squibb, and other Fortune 500 companies, as well as human resource and high-tech groups, government entities, universities, and more.

A regular invited speaker at international conferences on learning, humor, and business, Doni has appeared throughout the United States, and in Canada, Europe, and Southeast Asia. She has taught the HumorRulesR system through the University of California Extension.

Doni graduated magna cum laude from San Francisco State University with a degree in Broadcast Communications. She is a member of the American Society for Training and Development, the American Association for Therapeutic Humor, and the International Society for Humor Studies.

Doni Tamblyn can be contacted at:

HumorRules
P.O. Box 22575
Philadelphia PA 19110
Tel: (866) 700-1011/Local: (215) PEA SOUP (215) 732-7687)
Fax: (215) 732-7674
e-mail: *tamblyn@humorrules.com*
Web site: *www.HumorRules.com*